HOLINESS
AND
HEALING

DAN BOHI AND
DR. ROB MCCORKLE
FOREWORD BY COREY JONES

#becomingLOVE
media group
Bethany, Oklahoma

Becoming Love Ministries
7905 North West 48th Street
Bethany, OK 73008
BecomingLoveMinistries.com

During the writing of this book, Rob McCorkle was pastoring Crossroads Community
Church and was founder of Fire School Ministries. In 2018, Rob and Cindy resigned
from their church and dissolved Fire School to work fulltime with Becoming Love
Ministries. References to both ministries remain in this book for historical context.

The recorded conversations were transcribed by Karen Stout.

Acknowledgements

Dan wishes to thank the following:

- Debbie, my faithful partner and best friend, who has been with me for over thirty years in the good times and through the difficult seasons. I couldn't do what I do without her undying support. Together we've reared four wonderful children and soon to be thirteen grandchildren.
- Jim and Carolyn Bohi, my wonderful parents and prayer partners. My father spent more than thirty-five years in full-time ministry singing for the glory of God. He encourages me every night on the phone after my services.
- Dr. Don and Adeline Owens, former general superintendent in the Church of the Nazarene. They both exemplified holiness and healing in their ministry around the world. My father-in-law has been my personal theologian and sounding board for over thirty years.
- My friend Rob McCorkle who I've spoken to almost every single day for over five and a half years. We've talked about the Word, the Spirit, holiness, healing, and

everything in between. Our conversations have led to the writing of this book.

Rob wishes to thank the following:

-   Cindy, my best friend. I am so grateful for the sacrifices that she has made to fulfill the call upon our lives.
-   Bernadine McCorkle, my mother who at eighty-five years young prays for people to be healed at Walmart or McDonalds. She is still hungry for more of God's manifest presence and has set the bar high for me to follow when I reach her age.
-   Jess and Margaret Sellers, my wife's parents, who have consistently carried the torch of Jesus for more than fifty years without wavering.
-   Scott (and Kristi) Brown, Tami (and Jim) Dixon, and Kim (and Dave) Taucher, my senior staff at my church. They really do the work around Crossroads so that I can do the work around the nation.
-   The many friends who have poured into me, but especially Dan Bohi, Corey Jones, and Kevin Seymour.

ENDORSEMENTS

Dan Bohi and Rob McCorkle argue that a dove needs two functioning wings to fly. In the case of the Holy Spirit they point to purity and power, holiness and healing. How much longer will the church flop around on the ground with only one wing functional, debating with others over which wing is most important? And we wonder why the world is not attracted to a church that is hopping and flopping instead of flying and soaring!

Dr. Frank H. Billman
Director of Equipping Ministries, Aldersgate Renewal Ministries
Dean of the Methodist School for Supernatural Ministries
United Theological Seminary
Faculty Mentor for the Doctor of Ministry in Supernatural Ministry

In their new book, *Holiness and Healing*, Dan Bohi and Dr. Rob McCorkle have brought a fresh emphasis into our discussion of praying for healing. Bringing into the mix the holiness message of the Nazarene movement is a strong reminder that we cannot focus on ministry gifts without also pointing out the necessity of godly character, born out of intimacy with God. This book rightly teaches us that our healing ministries will be most influential and effective when gifts and character are married together, both being vitally important. I recommend all who are pursuing Kingdom ministry to absorb the message of this book.

Randy Clark
Overseer of the Apostolic Network
Global Awakening

Knowing Dan Bohi and Dr. Rob McCorkle personally many years, I love, affirm, and endorse them. They live what they pray and preach: real passion for Jesus, His Body, and the Spirit. They balance Bible messages of purity *and* power that produce holiness *and* healing. They pursue the Reviver for renewal in churches across the Body of Christ. Bohi and McCorkle help to fill a vacuum in the Holiness movement for resources about apostles, prophets, gifts of the Spirit, impartations, miracles, and manifestations. Many books that address these themes rarely embrace the need for heart purity, entire sanctification, and a life of holiness. Conversely, many books that address holiness of heart and life, rarely embrace themes such as apostles, prophets, gifts of the Spirit, impartations, miracles, and manifestations. In and through Dan and Rob, these biblical themes soar in practical fusion.

Daniel Ketchum, PhD
Global Servant of Yeshua/Jesus
Jerusalem, Israel

Working and writing through His uniquely called vessels, Dan Bohi and Rob McCorkle, I believe the Holy Spirit is offering our Nazarene tribe a revival. This fledgling revival, like hundreds of little lightning strikes, is springing up in church after church, manifesting as a resolute return to and revealing of *the* Nazarene Himself. Dan and Rob's new book, *Holiness and Healing*, invites us to sit at Jesus' feet (corporately and privately) so that we can walk as Jesus did, in purity and power while embodying His message, motives, maturity, and ministry. His divine power being manifest in corporate meetings and referenced in this book are signs that God is offering and waiting to revive our tribe that originally experienced both holiness and healing.

Hal Perkins

Itinerant Speaker

Founder of Heart Walk Ministries

I love Rob McCorkle! Once again, he has written a book that says what I have believed and practiced for decades, but he says it so much better than I ever could. Rob's combination of holiness roots, fiery passion for Jesus, careful scholarship, incredible knowledge of the Word, and desperate longing for purity and power have conspired together to produce a classic for the ages. I am thrilled to recommend this book to anyone who is serious about seeing the life and ministry of Jesus lived out in today's crazy world. How we need this book!

I not only love Dan Bohi, but I live with him! I travel full-time with Dan as his personal intercessor and partner in ministry. Simply put, there is no man on earth that I love and admire more than him. He is the real deal, and he lives Jesus 24/7/365 days a year. He shares Jesus with everyone we meet. He reads the entire Bible twice a month. He is fervently passionate about becoming love and living the life he describes in this book. Dan is the most Christ-like man that I know. He walks in daily anointing and the power of Jesus like no one I know. You will be blessed, challenged, convicted, and greatly encouraged by this book. Read it! Believe it! And by the power of Jesus, live it!

Craig Wesley Rench
Itinerant Intercessor with Dan Bohi Ministries

I have had the privilege of being Rob McCorkle's best friend for over thirty years. During this time I have watched him hunger for holiness and long for a continual heart transformation. I'm convinced that God has honored this hunger by allowing him to experience and then write the words of this book. He truly demonstrates what the life of a Christian looks like when they long to live with Power and Purity.

My friendship with Dan Bohi has impacted my life in eternal ways. Having travelled with Dan for weeks at a time has shown me the heart and passion of one who feeds himself on God's Word. I've personally witnessed the love and power of my heavenly Father through the ministry of Dan Bohi. The thoughts, revelation, and truth that they share in this book will mark me for the rest of my life. I encourage anyone that has a hunger for Christlikeness to invest the time to ingest the truths, challenges, and experiences that Dan and Rob share in these pages.

Kevin Seymour, Pastor
Lancaster, Ohio
Church of the Nazarene

CONTENTS

Foreword

In his book *Divine Healing*, Andrew Murray wrote, "The Holy Spirit in Jesus is a healing Spirit." It is this fundamental conviction that has spurred Dr. Rob McCorkle and Dan Bohi to enter into a revealing dialogue about such biblical topics as the work of the Holy Spirit, the power of prayer and impartation, the culture of the kingdom, the truth about divine healing, practical holiness, and other critical issues related to the Christian life and the Church.

As indicated in the title of the book, it is the fundamental conviction of these authors that there is an inextricable connection between holiness and healing, that without holiness there is no sustained healing and without healing, holiness is incomplete. Truly this connection between holiness and healing goes all the way back to John Wesley, who spoke of holiness as the healing of the sin diseased soul. In his sermon "Original Sin," Wesley wrote, "What is the proper religion of Jesus Christ? It is the healing of the soul. The great Physician of souls applies medicines to heal this sickness; to restore human nature, totally corrupted."

Dr. Rob McCorkle and Dan Bohi have devoted their lives and ministry to the restoration of what Dan refers to as "the two wings of the Dove." It is the belief that the Holy Spirit's work should result in both purity and power, in spiritual gifts and the fruit of the Spirit, and in holiness and miracles in and through the lives of believers. Dan and Rob have witnessed firsthand the power of the Holy Spirit to impart holiness and healing to countless people's lives throughout their ministries. What makes this book truly significant is that the authors share firsthand testimonies and stories about miracles, healing, and holiness in the lives of people. I am personally a witness and recipient of the power of impartation through Dan and Rob's ministry and friendship. It is my sincere and fervent prayer that this book gets into the hands of pastors and people who are longing for a revolutionary revival of the Shekinah glory in the Church, resulting in kingdom transformation of communities, cities, and nations.

I leave you with a convicting call from one of the first general superintendents of the Church of the Nazarene. In a sermon entitled, "The Secret Place of Prayer," J. W. Goodwin once said, "The early church exercised healing by the Spirit and power of divine presence, or supernatural healing through faith in His name; the commission has never been changed, but continued through the centuries until the present. Thank God, there is a much wider manifestation of this power and presence among believers, and will increase until the very end."

— Corey Jones, Senior Pastor, Crossroads Tabernacle, Fort Worth, Texas

INTRODUCTION

In January of 2007, I took a seven-week sabbatical from the church where I was the senior leader. I left my church with no plans of returning. The church was about nine years old after my wife and I began the church plant with fourteen people in a high school auditorium. Through a series of events, mostly well intentioned programs orchestrated by talent and personality, I was spent spiritually and emotionally. What was worse, I hadn't sensed the voice of the Holy Spirit for almost two years.

I developed a new definition of hell just prior to my sabbatical: hell is wherever the Spirit of God is absent. I don't want to minimize the fact that there is an eternal hell prepared for the devil and his angels (see Matthew 25:41), but I felt isolated and paralyzed listening to my own voice. Darkness surrounded me, and I believe whenever we are far from hearing Him, we're in trouble. So I left my church with the intentions of not only resigning but also getting out of full-time ministry.

Something amazing happened to me during my sabbatical, however, that changed everything. I had an encounter with God, and He won! I was undone for several days in His presence, and when I returned home, I wanted everyone in my church to experience the manifest presence of Jesus like I had. Within several months, almost everyone in my church did have that experience. Needless to say, we no longer had the same church. Oh, it was the same building and the same people, but the Holy Spirit rearranged everything from the music, the messages, the prayers, the announcements, to the entire format.

We went from being totally focused on attracting seekers to becoming radically focused on attracting His presence. Our greatest desire then, and now, was to experience the *manifest* presence of God, not just the omnipresence. Jesus says that He will "manifest" Himself to those He loves (see John 14:21). That means He will intensify His presence. He will reveal Himself in ways that we've never experienced if we're hungry for Him to show Himself off.

Week after week and month after month the presence of the Lord was demonstrated in ways I hadn't experienced before—and in ways that I hadn't been prepared for in my formal education. If I have to be honest, most of what we were experiencing after my sabbatical was ridiculed and criticized by the traditional educational system. I had heard stories of "denominational witch hunts" of sorts that sought to remove the credentials of those who operated in the supernatural manifestations of the Holy Spirit. So I was not only unprepared for what God was doing in my church, but I couldn't share stories with too many people in my denomination.

And let me add, we had many stories to share! We actually saw people healed by the power of God! Diseases were cured, sickness was taken away, and bodies were restored to health. We saw people delivered from demonic oppression and strongholds. We witnessed people being born again, and many believers had their hearts purified by the same power of God that had delivered them from emotional, mental, and spiritual bondage. We experienced all nine of the manifestations in 1 Corinthians 12:8–10, but they didn't cause division or dissention like I had always been told. Rather, they manifested for the profit of the entire body (see 1 Corinthians 12:7). Our church was blessed and benefitted by the Spirit's graces. Nevertheless, right or wrong, we flew beneath the radar for several years because of my fear to share with others what God was doing.

My longtime friend, then and now, was the only person that I spoke with about it—at least within the Church of the Nazarene. Kevin Seymour pastored a Nazarene church about an hour from me, and we would frequently meet for lunch. My stories weren't met with resistance from him but with a bit of skepticism only because He had been schooled along with me, and we didn't have a paradigm (wine skin) for what was happening in my church.

About a year after my encounter, Kevin started experiencing "signs and wonders" in his church. It started with an extraordinary healing of his son, and after that, the Holy Spirit poured out amazing things in his life and ministry. To this day Kevin testifies to seeing God do extraordinary things. God is still doing amazing things through Kevin's life and ministry. Our lunches together, after the Holy Spirit fell on his church, became iron sharpening iron (see Proverbs 27:17). But outside of Kevin, my knowledge of those who functioned in the extraordinary power and supernatural gifts of the Holy Spirit within our denomination was limited.

Three years after my sabbatical, in the spring of 2010, I was holding a meeting in Sunbury, Ohio. I arrived at the church about an hour early and felt prompted to call my friend and Nazarene evangelist Chuck Millhuff. Chuck and I have talked with each other since the early 80s, and he was aware of what I was experiencing in my life and ministry. During that particular conversation I talked about experiencing a prophetic anointing. I told him about a specific healing that occurred through a word of knowledge. That's when he said to me, "You need to talk with Dan Bohi. You both speak the same language."

I had never heard of him. I knew his father Jim Bohi, who spent most of his life in song evangelism in the Church of the Nazarene, but I had no knowledge of Dan Bohi. Chuck went on to describe Dan. He said, "I have never heard anyone who knows the Word of God like this guy. He has read the Bible over sixty times, and his memory of the Word is stunning. He's experienced miracles, signs, and wonders in his meetings — everything you have and more. In fact, he hugged me the other day, and I felt electricity surge through my body. You've simply got to meet him."

I was intrigued, but what *really* captured my attention was the fact that Dan was a member in the Church of the Nazarene. I thought to myself, how is this guy getting away with all this stuff? And why hadn't I heard of him? About a month later my district superintendent, Trevor Johnston, sent a report out that had circulated throughout all the superintendents in the Church of the Nazarene. A meeting with Dan Bohi had taken place in Bronx, New York, at the Bronx Bethany Church of the Nazarene under the leadership of Dr. Samuel Vassel.

This report told of mass confessions, supernatural healings, and extraordinary deliverances that took place in a service lasting nearly six hours. I was stunned that this e-mail had been sent and even more intrigued by this guy named Dan Bohi. Who was this mysterious full-time evangelist who functioned in the power of the Holy Spirit? Within a few weeks, I sent a private Facebook message to Dan explaining who I was and what God was doing in my life and ministry, and I told him that we had a mutual friend named Chuck Millhuff. About a month later Dan called me, and we talked on the phone for nearly two hours.

That first conversation with Dan was certainly not the last one that we've had. Since 2010, we have studied God's Word together, have swapped message ideas, and have preached together in revivals and conferences. I've had the blessing of watching the ministry of Dan Bohi firsthand. I've watched him preach, minister, weep, and cry out for pastors and churches. I've observed a growth pattern in his life of downward mobility—a path that is leading him to deeper experiences of humility and greater experiences of love. I know his strengths, and I also know his weaknesses. I am aware of what makes him laugh and what makes him cry. I am honored to know him and call him my friend, and I'm blessed to have the privilege to write this book with him.

I can honestly tell you that I've rarely met anyone like him. His love and knowledge of God's Word is almost incomparable. Nearly every single day since 2008, he soaks in the Bible. For several years he read the Bible through every single month. One year he read the Gospels and book of Acts over sixty times. His prayers and messages are a barrage of Scripture. His devotion to the Word is only equaled by his belief in what it says. Dan doesn't read the Bible with a critical eye looking for apparent errors. He reads the Bible as a timeless message and expects to encounter the Holy Spirit who inspired every word. The Bible to him is a description of what we should expect to experience, and that's especially true with the book of Acts.

Dan also functions freely in the supernatural gifts of the Holy Spirit. I've observed his sensitive devotion to the leadership of the Spirit in services, and I've watched the power of God flow from him as he has laid hands on people in ministry lines. I have seen people get out of wheelchairs, throw their crutches on the floor, dance in liberation of pain, and remove leg braces to run around the church. I've heard him prophesy over people with pinpoint accuracy and describe things about their lives that only God could have known. He moves in the power of the Holy Spirit as the apostles and early believers did as recorded in the book of Acts and early church history. It's not worked up emotionalism either. In fact, he's a bit cautious of the fanfare that accompanies many of the crusades today, so he doesn't distribute excessive reports of miraculous healings through Internet and e-mail.

Dan's ministry is a unique balance and fusion of purity and power. Nearly every meeting he conducts he moves in signs, wonders, and supernatural gifts. Healings and miracles follow him as Jesus promised in Mark 16. But he also calls people to a life of holiness. In fact, that's the foundation in Dan's mind that sustains a supernatural culture. Sanctification to Dan is not a Nazarene message but a biblical experience that everyone could and should have. I've watched people run forward in Pentecostal churches to die to themselves and have their hearts purified by the same power of the Spirit that healed their bodies. I've watched hundreds, even thousands, of people weep and experience a side of God that they didn't know was possible — namely, that they could have their hearts cleansed from the essence and power of sin.

We've both had our share of criticisms over the last few years, but I've watched a love and grace well up in Dan's heart toward those who have leveled complaints against him. He hasn't relinquished his pursuit of God either. His response is still the same, "I have a calling to wake up the Church, and I can't quit," he says. So from 2008 to this day, Dan has crisscrossed the United States several times and has witnessed many thousands of conversions, healings, miracles, signs, and wonders. He hasn't been deterred by critics, physical challenges, financial issues, or personal and family concerns. He's remained faithful to the call of God in his life. Moreover, his hunger and desperation to encounter more of Jesus is only intensifying.

About a year ago we started talking about the vacuum that exists in the Church of the Nazarene for books and resources that address the topics in this book. If we're honest, there aren't too many books on pastor's shelves in Nazarene churches dealing with apostles, supernatural gifts, impartations, miracles, and manifestations. The reasons for that are addressed in this book. We were equally concerned for other denominations, too. There *are* books in certain denominations that address the subjects of miracles, signs, and wonders, and they speak of apostles, prophets, and extraordinary gifts. But they rarely mention the need for heart purity, a life of holiness, and sanctification, and that is equally concerning in our minds and hearts.

We believe that the message of the Bible is both purity *and* power. We believe that Jesus' ministry established holiness *and* healing. So the topics addressed in the book are not aimed at one particular denomination but rather to the entire Church of Jesus Christ. Our desire to see revival is not merely for one church or denomination, but we long to see renewal throughout the entire body of Christ. So we believe that this book will be a source of encouragement to believers of every church and tribe. That being said, hopefully it will give permission to those in the Church of the Nazarene and other traditional Holiness churches to explore the subjects that we address. The contents of each chapter are both biblical and essential to the ongoing life and ministry of the local church and to the spiritual life of every pastor, leader, and layperson who reads it.

This book transpired through several conversations in hotel rooms, and we made a list of topics that we've both encountered or have discussed with pastors, leaders, and laypeople across the United States. We decided that I would interview Dan, and the contents of each chapter would contain the discussions that followed. I agreed to write a brief introduction and conclusion to each chapter. In May of 2015 we made a makeshift studio at my church, and we spent three and a half hours recording our conversations. Without trying to sound overdramatic, the power and presence of God rested upon us both during the recording sessions. There were times when we paused to wipe the tears from our eyes. We believe that you will sense that same presence of the Holy Spirit as you read each page.

Neither of us are experts in church ministry, nor are we attempting to set mandates for every pastor and leader to follow. We don't have all the answers, and in some cases we have *no* answers. Much of what's been written about is our experiences and even some of our own questions. Beyond that we desired to explore the unexplored with this book, especially within the Holiness movement. There are facets of the Bible that people either avoid or dismiss from their ministries and vocabulary. Much of that is due to fear and ignorance. Religious paradigms and old wine skins have kept many of us from experiencing greater things with God; therefore, we settle for much less in the kingdom of God than what could be experienced. We hope that this book will change that and open the door to a spirit of revelation in your life, and we believe that if you read it with an open heart, you will be inspired to pursue deeper encounters with Christ and His Word.

Finally, we hope that you will experience a touch by the Holy Spirit at the end of this book. Dan prayed a prayer of impartation at the end of our recording session, and when he finished, we both felt that the Holy Spirit was going to touch, heal, inspire, and encourage thousands of people who read it. So find a sweet spot to read this book and enjoy the journey.

Chapter One

A JOURNEY INTO FAITH

In the fall of 1982, during a camp meeting service, I went forward in front one thousand people during the invitation at the end of the message. The speaker asked who desired to totally consecrate their lives to God with no strings attached. This was a clear invitation to allow God to sanctify our hearts through and through. That evening, I literally laid my body over the altar and told God that I was a blank sheet of paper. He was free to fill in the blanks. I relinquished my life, and He filled me with Himself.

It was only months after that event when the Holy Spirit called me into a preaching ministry. He specifically commissioned me, and I started preaching in 1983 and haven't turned away. Even after the initial call to ministry, God has called me to fulfill specific mandates along the way. It still amazes me that God chooses to use people to accomplish divine tasks. He is fully capable of doing whatever He desires without the aid of human assistance, yet He links Himself to people like you and me. Throughout biblical history men and woman have been used by God to fulfill what would be impossible assignments without His power and grace.

The fact is God calls us all to accomplish significant ministries for His kingdom. Every born again, Spirit–filled believer has been called by God. There is no getting around the commission accounts in the New Testament. They apply to every single person reading them. When Jesus commissioned His disciples, He was calling you and me to fulfill a mission, and an essential mission I might add. Jesus' commission accounts are universal calls to all believers, but God has *specific* assignments for each individual, too. Those specific calls are unique to the person being called and the assignment will not look like anyone else.

The apostle Paul, though commissioned like the disciples to evangelize, had a very specific call that was uniquely designed for him. His call started in an encounter with God in Acts chapter nine and was tailored in Acts 13:46, when he turned his attention to preaching to Gentiles. Paul the persecutor became Paul the proclaimer. And both Jews and Gentiles not only heard the Word of God, but they also saw the power of God through Paul's hands.

Moreover, God often calls those who feel inadequate for the assignment because this increases their dependency upon God. People who feel foolish, weak, and despised are the very ones that God targets (see 1 Corinthians 1:27–28). It's just like God to call someone that we would least expect and then to fulfill something through him that we would least anticipate. Every specific call is conditioned upon our personal response. No doubt we can refuse Him who speaks (see Hebrews 12:25), but that is not advisable for many reasons. God isn't looking for qualified people, but He will qualify the people He calls when we respond affirmatively to His bidding. He's really only looking for one response from each of us, and that is "yes."

Dan Bohi was faced with a simple question from God that required a "yes," and his response has led Him on an unforgettable mission so far. I have often said that Dan is an anomaly. That word means something that is out of the ordinary. Dan didn't enter ministry through the ranks of most. He didn't graduate from a Bible college or complete a seminary degree. He never intended on spending his life as an itinerant preacher whose one purpose is to wake up the Church of Jesus Christ. My reason for stating that is not to discourage anyone from attending school or from pursuing a formal education. I merely tell you that to encourage you.

If you didn't have the privilege to gain a formal education, or if you didn't grow up in the church, or if you didn't know the "right" people, then take courage because none of that really matters in the final analysis. God will use anyone who will obey Him without conditions. He will use the educated and uneducated alike. He will use the talented and untalented just the same, and He will use anyone with any background from any family from any nation. God is only looking for those who will say yes to Him when He calls. My interview with Dan began by talking about his journey into faith. As you read this chapter, I pray that God will not only challenge you to a deeper level of faith, but I pray that you will say yes to whatever He bids you to do.

Rob: It's great to be with you today, Dan, and I'm excited about what we are going to be talking about. I'm also excited about what God is doing in our lives and in our ministries. Dan, you have literally crisscrossed this nation time and time again preaching the gospel. So, I want to begin with your journey into faith. Talk to me about your accident and how your life took a pivotal change at that point.

Dan: I was reared obviously with great Christian parents and came to be a believer in Jesus Christ at the age of fourteen. I immediately had great passion, zeal, and excitement about my faith. I seemed to have an ability to really walk with Jesus and I wanted my light to shine wherever I went. I married my high school sweetheart and started a successful business. But as time evolved, I noticed that there was an inner struggle with things in my life that I didn't like.

Rob: Like what, for example?

Dan: Things like pride, lust, and fear. I sought the baptism of the Holy Spirit many times. I sought the deep work of sanctification over and over again looking for something to change, but

I never seemed to have enough faith to accept it. After several years of seeking to be sanctified and never feeling something that was a real–life change, I gave up hope for it. That moment, I believe, is when compromise and sin entered back into my life.

I went through about fifteen years of what I would call a "wilderness" or "winter" experience. I didn't leave church, I didn't cease desiring to go to heaven, but there was no power, no peace, and no confidence in my life. Church was just something that I did because I wanted my children and my family to know God, but in reality I didn't really know Him the way my parents did. So in 1995, I started really praying a serious prayer to God. I said, "Lord, if you cannot change me and give me this power I read about in the Bible — this peace, confidence, and boldness, then I would rather die than live this miserable existence."

Rob: Okay, that's a pretty serious prayer that I've heard other people tell me they prayed, but did God take you at your word?

Dan: Yes! On June 14, 1995, I came home from work and my wife Debbie had given me some news that was discouraging, and I remember that

I collapsed on the kitchen table. I felt like I had nothing left to give. It was some sort of a breakdown. I don't know how extensive it was, but I do remember looking at my wife and she said, "Why don't you just give up and trust God with your life." I went to bed that night and I usually don't remember dreams, but I had an extremely vivid dream that night. In my dream, I was hanging on the edge of a cliff and I felt like I was going to fall to my death. Right below me was Jesus, and He said, "Let go, I'll catch you if you just let go." I remember in my dream that I was too afraid to let go. I thought that I had to fix myself first before I could trust Jesus with my entire life.

When I woke up, I started my day as I had done for years. At that time, I was a carpenter and had a framing crew. I headed to work to finish a basement with my crew in Amber Meadows. On the way to Ashton Estates in Olathe, Kansas, I took a left turn and a 60,000 pound truck smashed into the side of my pickup. It actually came through the passenger side and hit me with the bumper of the truck, and it pushed me through the driver's side. I broke my back, broke my pelvis, lacerated my liver, and tore my urethra out of my bladder. It just crushed my whole midsection. I had been praying that if God couldn't change me, then He could just take my life. I certainly don't think that

30

God caused that truck to hit me, but I think He allowed it to occur for His purpose.

It was a long day at the hospital. They kept doing tests, trying to figure out what was wrong with me. Throughout the day, and I can't tell you how many times, I could see myself lying on the gurney from above. A man kept grabbing my shirt and saying, "Don't leave us, Brother Dan, we aren't done with you yet." As he would do that, I would feel myself going back into my body, and this happened over and over again. I kept asking the nurses for pain medication, and I remember them saying, "We can't give you anything until we find out everything that is wrong." So I just kept leaving my body and hearing this person tell me not to leave earth.

Rob: Do you think it was an angel?

Dan: I think it was, Rob, because my mom had been praying for me for a long time. He would come to me and repeatedly say, "We aren't done with you." After all the tests were completed, they finally got me into the ICU. My wife was sitting beside my bed as I just lay there. They had me hooked up to all kinds of IV's and oxygen, and they put a catheter in my stomach which I actually had for thirteen months. I remember Debbie saying, "There are a lot of visitors who want to see you." Yet, I couldn't muster up the strength and courage to see anyone because I was too afraid. For my entire life up until that point, and I was thirty-four at that time, I had always been able to place a mask of confidence and strength on to cover up my insecurities and fears.

That night in the ICU, however, I had no strength to put on my mask. I told Debbie that I was too afraid to see anybody because I was unable to walk and I couldn't work. I was in such fear at the time that I didn't even know how I was going to make it. I remember just looking up and saying, "Jesus, I'm not going to make it, am I?" Then I looked to my left and saw the heart monitor, and I saw it go flat. The time was 5:37 p.m. This time that man didn't grab me by the shirt and say, "Don't leave us, we aren't done with you." This time Jesus came up to my bed, and He was standing right next to my wife. He spoke two things to me. First, He said, "Son, I have forgiven your sins." It was like the first time in my life I realized that I didn't have to earn forgiveness. I had such an incredible peace with God. Jesus had forgiven my sins and I had great comfort in that fact.

But He didn't stop with the first statement. His second statement was a question—He simply asked, "When will you trust me with your life, Dan?" When I look back on it now, almost twenty years later, the night before my accident my wife had asked, "Why don't you give up and trust God." Then I had that dream where Jesus was right below me on the cliff saying, "Let go, I'll catch you." So, there I was less than twenty-four hours later, and Jesus was asking me the same question, "When will you trust me with your life?" I didn't even have to hesitate because I was in His presence. My immediate response was, "Yes!" That was all I said, and it seemed like Jesus opened me up at that moment and took out all of my anxiety, all my fears, all my lust, all my pride, and everything unlike Him. He took it out of me, but He didn't leave me empty. He completely filled me up with Himself.

I remember when I woke up and tried to yell, "It's okay; Jesus is here," yet I couldn't talk because they had me on morphine. I tried so hard to proclaim that Jesus was there. My wife was crying while I tried to explain to her what had happened. I managed to say, "Honey, we aren't going to be homeless. Jesus has come to me, He talked to me, and He is inside of me." My wife couldn't understand it, but that was a defining moment in my life I have never recovered from. That was an encounter with Jesus.

Rob: What happened next?

Dan: My first reaction was that I wanted to see my visitors now. I wanted to see them because I had no fear. As I think back on my life, that was the first time I felt no fear. I couldn't walk, I couldn't work, and I didn't know what was going to come of my life, but I knew that Jesus inside of me was greater than what I was going through. I had absolutely no fear. I experienced perfect love filling me, casting out all fear. I remember looking at my nurses and being worried about them. That wasn't normal for me! Yet everything had changed, and now I was concerned for them.

I didn't know it at the time, but that was one of the first evidences that my nature and my heart were different. I actually thought about others more than myself. God changed my desires, Rob. I didn't even know all that had happened inside my heart—all I know is that I said yes! I trusted Jesus with my entire life. That first week in the hospital many different people came to visit me. I had the privilege of leading seven people to Christ while I was in the hospital. I had never done that before, yet there was this powerful anointing in my heart. And I wanted everyone to have the same Jesus that I had.

Rob: What about when you were released from the hospital?

Dan: When I was released, I had to learn how to walk again, so I used a walker. I wasn't able to get out much, but I was anxious to see people because I wanted them to know Jesus like I knew Him. People would come to my home, and I would share with them about Jesus coming to me and talking with me, filling me, and being in me. I told them how He took away my fear and cleansed my heart. Sometimes people would look at me like I had two heads. They couldn't understand the change because they had all known the old Dan Bohi before the accident, but it was different and I could hardly explain it.

This might sound strange, but I would hope and wish that things would go wrong with my house so that people would have to come visit me so I could witness to them! I had never been that way before. My whole life had been driven by trying to succeed and build a business and participate in sports, enjoying all the things that *I* could do, and now my focus and passion was on giving people this Jesus who had come to me and filled me. A friend said that I should start going into prisons to share the Word. I couldn't believe the response. I just shared out of the joy and overflow of my life. So many people came to faith, Rob, I couldn't believe it. It was amazing!

This joy and passion didn't stop, either. Everyone I knew in the construction industry and those in my life who lived in Olathe, Kansas, heard my story over and over again. God gave me the privilege of leading 181 people to Jesus in the first six months of being released from the hospital.

I remember they asked our family to sing at College Church of the Nazarene. J. K. Warrick, my pastor, was so excited when I brought 200 visitors to church that fall. It was hard to believe how much passion I had for people to know Jesus. Listen, I didn't get that from studying. I got that by an encounter. I still didn't understand fully what had happened, but I look back now and Acts 1:8 says, "But you will receive power when the Holy Spirit has come upon you; and you shall be My witnesses both in Jerusalem, and in all Judea and Samaria, and even to the remotest part of the earth." I know now that what that verse says is what happened to me, even though at the time I didn't comprehend it.

Rob: Dan, what do you think happened to you when Jesus came to your side at the hospital?

Dan: Two years after that experience in the hospital bed, I was praying in my private time. This would have been the summer of 1997. I was asking God what He did to me. I wanted to know what happened because it was *not* wearing off— it was actually intensifying. It wasn't an emotional experience, but rather it was a defining transformational experience. Life didn't end with that encounter, but rather it opened up a door and life actually began. I didn't know what it was because I wasn't at church when the encounter occurred. I just said, "Yes!"

Finally the Lord responded to me, and He said, "Son, that is when I purified your heart." I remember that I was stunned and I said, "Jesus, everyone needs this; it is the only thing that works." It was like I was trying to give Jesus advice, which is ludicrous when I think about it, but I was so taken back that I had experienced this sanctifying work. I had walked in it for two years and I didn't even know what it was. I just knew that I had an insatiable love for God and for people, and because of the filling of the Holy Spirit, I was fulfilling the greatest commandment—I was telling everyone about Jesus.

Yet, it wasn't out of duty—it was out of passion. I'm so thankful that God gave me that experience. I shared it with all my friends. I told them that they really could be sanctified because it had happened to me. Within about a year all of my kids, who were teenagers at the time, and my siblings, my wife, and my cousins prayed to be sanctified. It seemed like everyone around me was affected by this powerful Holy Spirit encounter. When I looked back, all I had said was "Yes," but, like the Lord said to Zerubbabel, "'Not by might nor by power, but by My Spirit,' says the Lord of hosts" (Zechariah 4:6).

Rob: That's so amazing. You couldn't stop telling people about it, could you?

Dan: Not at all. I started sharing it with friends at work and started leading men into the sanctifying work of the Spirit, into the baptism of the Holy Spirit. We started a men's group that outgrew houses, and finally we all agreed to build a barn on my little farm, which they called the "Glory Barn." We met there every Wednesday for nine years. Sometimes there would be up to 200 men that would show up, and all we talked about was being baptized and filled with the Holy Spirit because it was the only thing that worked.

I couldn't believe it, but men in their 80s to teen-agers, from Catholics to Charismatics to Nazarenes, everybody came from all walks of life and all races, creeds, and colors. The Holy Spirit didn't separate us. He unified us. We had one passion, and that was for Him to be glorified in our lives so that the world would be changed around us. This went on for nine years. The passion for His Word was unquenchable. There would be days where I couldn't get out of His Word. I just loved Him so much I had to know more about Him.

Rob: All of this was happening while you had your construction company. How was that working?

Dan: Well, by 2005, I was hoping for a break. The business was growing, my family was getting older, but I was still traveling on the weekends and sharing the gospel. We were seeing great things happening. People were being born again, sanctified, and healed, yet I didn't understand where all this was taking me. Besides, I was consumed by work as well as taking care of my family.

So in 2006, I just took some time off. At that time, our business had just tripled in size, but there was a longing in my heart for more of the Spirit. I wasn't satisfied with the business any longer. Interestingly, in 2007, the housing market crashed, and my wife and I lost everything we had ever accumulated. We thought that we had made it in this American dream of success and security, but when the housing market crashed, all that was taken from us. We didn't know what to do. All we had ever known was construction.

Rob: You told me that you lost a lot of money when the market crashed.

Dan: Oh my, we lost millions of dollars, all of our properties, and our ability to do our business was gone. Yet it was different because there was still a "knowing" inside of my spirit that God was with me even though I couldn't understand why we had lost so much. I remember asking God, "What do you want me to do now?" Listen, we honestly didn't know how we were going to live because there were no resources left. We had sold everything that we had to try to keep things afloat. We didn't have anything left to sell except for one red pickup truck, and that was it. From having millions of dollars and hundreds of properties to one red pickup, that was what we were reduced to. So I wanted to know what God wanted me to do with my life.

I remember His response. It is still kind of eerie, but it was very simple. He said, "Buy a Bible and read it again." I thought that is the craziest advice I had ever heard, yet I believe life is in His voice, and I was looking for a word. I was asking what was I to do at the age of forty-eight, and I had nothing left except to obey His voice. So I bought a New King James Bible, and I remember that I read it through in two weeks because I was so desperate to find out what to do with my life. I had no clue what I was going to do.

My wife and I had nothing—no security, nothing to fall back on, and we had cashed in everything we had ever accumulated—it was all gone. During those two weeks when I read the Bible through, we had gone out of town to sit in front of some mountains to pray and seek the Lord. While on the way back, I stopped at a Shell station in Laramie, Wyoming, to get gas. The date was October 10, 2008. It was about 2:30 in the afternoon. I was longing to hear from God because I had read the whole Bible through, and I didn't feel any clear direction on my future.

As I hung up the gas pump, I felt the Spirit come upon me at that moment, and He said, "I want you to preach the gospel until you die." Then He gave me my mission statement, "I want you to wake up the Church of Jesus Christ through the power, the purity, and the freedom to the

Spirit–filled life as experienced and exhibited in the lives of the believers in the book of Acts."

Rob: Wow! That's so amazing, Dan.

Dan: He gave me all that right there at the gas pump. I remember Debbie coming back from the restroom, and I said that I believe God just called me to preach full–time. Her response was, "Are you serious?" I just laughed and said, "That will teach you to go to the restroom, honey." We had no idea what that entailed. God just said that He wanted me to preach the gospel until I died. I didn't know if that meant that I was sick and only had a few weeks to live, or if God had a way to accomplish this because I had no training or formal education. I had only read lots of books and read my Bible.

Rob: This is funny when you think about it because you didn't have any meetings scheduled at that time.

Dan: No, I didn't have any meetings scheduled. In fact, I didn't even have an idea how to schedule a meeting. I just had a call from God. I called my daddy and told him about God's call in my life, and he affirmed the call. I called Chuck Millhuff, Dave Felter, my pastor J. K Warrick, and all of them affirmed the call. I called my brother who was a partner in our business, and he said, "Dan, you need to go for it." I didn't know what all was involved in this call or how to do it.

We just started having prayer meetings and invited all these saints that I believed in, such as Gerry Holman, Evelyn Gibson, Dr. Gordon Wetmore, Dr. and Mrs. Don Owens — who are my in-laws, my parents, my brother, my wife, and all of these saints that I knew — about twenty in all. And we started praying that God would give me a way to preach and minister. We prayed for open doors.

In one of those prayer meetings, my dad said, "We shouldn't pray for meetings, but we should pray that when you get a meeting, it would be a good one." I thought, *Dad, that is easy for you to say, but I don't have much time here.* Well, I got a call from a friend, Nowel George, who was pastoring in Monet, Missouri. He asked if I could come to his church in two weeks. I remember saying, "Well, let me check my schedule." I didn't have a schedule. I had no meetings lined up, so I called him back and said that was perfect. Nowel's church was my first revival meeting.

Rob: So, let me get this straight. He asked you for a meeting, and you said that you had to check your schedule?

Dan: I did. I don't know why I said that. I guess that I didn't want to act like I didn't have anything going on. That was the first of November in 2008. Since that time I have preached in over 700 churches in the last six years and seven months. We have been in forty-two states, and this year the Lord told me not to keep track of statistics anymore; however, when I stopped keeping track, I had seen over 150,000 people come to altars to be sanctified.

Rob: Oh my word, that's so awesome!

Dan: I have always let the district superintendents or the pastors send reports simply because God told me to do that in the beginning. To date, I think there are over 32,000 people who have testified to being healed physically. This all started with a call at a gas station in Laramie, Wyoming.

Rob: Let's go back to that. We were traveling together last year and as we journeyed through Laramie, Wyoming, we stopped at that same gas station. It is kind of an ominous spot when you look at it. I believe I took a picture of that pump.

Dan: You did. I carry that in my journal now. Every day when I write in my journal about my journey with Jesus, I see that picture of the gas pump. On the back of the picture, I wrote that this is where I received my call to wake up the church.

Rob: I want to go back to something else. When you came out of the hospital and you were sharing your faith, being zealous for the gospel, you were still using a walker, correct?

Dan: Yes, I had to use a walker for about three months after the accident because of my broken pelvis and back.

Rob: So even in that condition, your zeal for God didn't wane. Nothing else mattered but Jesus.

Dan: All I had was zeal and passion. I didn't even know where it was coming from except that it was getting hotter.

Rob: Tell me about that night when you were actually physically healed. I think it's humorous.

Dan: Oh yes, I forgot to share about that. I had several surgeries during the recovery time of six months. I think it was three different surgeries. After one of the surgeries, I was lying in a hospital bed at home. (I had to sleep on a hospital bed because of my back and pelvis.) I was watching a TV show and this man named James Robison, was talking about how God could heal people if they believed. It was around 2 o'clock in the morning and Debbie was asleep next to me on the regular bed. The Holy Spirit spoke to me and said, "I've healed your emotions, I've healed your spirit, I've given you a call, I've taken care of your family, and you are not homeless." And I said, "Yes, Lord you have done all that."

Then He specifically said to me, "I can heal your body if you just reach out and touch me." I thought, *How do I do that?* I just felt like I should raise my arms up, but it felt so strange. But I did it anyways. I just lifted up my hands in the middle of the night, and in the moment that I raised my hands I felt warm tingles go all the way down through my body. I was able to get out of the hospital bed and walk without my walker.

Rob: Praise God, Dan.

Dan: I had no pain. They never had to do surgery on my pelvis again because it shifted into place at that moment. I got up and walked downstairs. I had a catheter in my stomach, so I had a bag that hung on my belt line, but I walked fourteen steps downstairs in my pajamas and I had no pain. I started laughing right there in the middle of the night. I remember looking around the house for things to do. My wife had been doing so much of the work taking care of the kids and trying to take care of me. I started dusting the furniture at 2 o'clock in the morning. I don't dust, but that night I started dusting furniture, and I was watering her plants, too.

Debbie came downstairs and was wondering what was going on. I told her that God had touched me and that I had no pain! We both started to cry, and then we started dancing together. It was so funny because we were in our pajamas, and we both had morning breath. It was 2 o'clock in the morning, yet we were dancing around our living room because God took away my pain. When that happened, I started believing that God not only could heal a person's soul, but He could actually heal a person's body. You can't talk someone out of that once they've experienced it.

Rob: Yeah, that was really the genesis of the healing ministry that was birthed in you.

Dan: Yes, it was.

Rob: Amen. Praise God for that experience, Dan. What a wonderful journey your life has taken up to this point.

As we conclude this chapter, my thoughts are directed toward two things that were discussed. First, when Dan opened his heart up to God while in the hospital, God cleansed his heart through and through. All his fears, pride, anxiety, and lust were purified. Only God can do that! He has the power to not only heal the body, but He can cleanse our hearts from the stench of sin. God prepared His vessel. He made Dan into a vessel of honor (see 2 Timothy 2:20–21).

Holiness is not a byproduct we can take or leave, and it's not a doctrine contrived in the minds of certain denominations. Holiness is a biblical message and it is possible for the Holy Spirit to enter our hearts and cleanse us through and through (see 1 Thessalonians 5:23). We don't have to work ourselves into this and we don't have to jump through religious hoops. God is only looking for those who will yield their entire lives to Him. I believe that God desires to open us all up and take out fear, pride, jealousy, insecurity, lust, anger, or whatever sin might be buried within. You don't have to work yourself into this experience, you only need to open your heart up to the Holy Spirit and let Him do the work.

Second, I believe all of us are presented with those defining moments in our lives where God comes to us and singles us out for a specific purpose. The Bible is replete with examples of this. Samuel was summoned by God when he was young,

Jeremiah was called while in his mother's womb, Isaiah had an encounter while in the temple, and Mary was approached by the Lord to become the birth mother of Jesus. These are but a few examples of God's unique, specific call upon an individual to complete a divine assignment.

I could take people to the places in my life where God spoke to me about specific assignments. I've been in parks, church sanctuaries, coffee shops, twenty thousand feet in the air while on a plane, or sometimes sitting in a car at a traffic light. Some of these moments when God singled me out have been dramatic where I sensed the overwhelming presence of the Lord rest upon me, and other times I've sensed the still small voice of the Holy Spirit speaking to me. But in each case, God was looking for an affirmative response from me. God wanted me to say yes to His call—yes to His assignment.

No one is exempt. God desires to use His people, and He will use them in grand ways and in simple tasks. Sometimes when we hear about other people's call into a particular ministry, we hang our heads and accept the lie that what God has asked of us isn't that important. Let me assure you that is not true. Whatever God has asked of us carries with it eternal significance, and while my life or your life won't look like Dan's, or anyone else's for that matter, God will use you in profound ways you may not see this side of eternity. He is looking for workers in the vineyard because the harvest is ripe. He will single you out. He will come to you probably time and time again. But you must answer His call. You must be willing to trust God with everything. Jesus asked Peter if he would be willing to lay down his life (see John 13:38). One encounter with God can change your life forever and it can change the lives of those you minister to. But you must be willing to lay your life down for Jesus. You must be willing to say yes to Him with no conditions. And when you do, when you say, "Here I am," your journey will begin.

Chapter Two

THE NECESSITY OF PURITY AND POWER

Irecently wrote a book entitled, *Bridging the Great Divide: Reuniting Word and Spirit.* The book addressed the division that occurred just over one hundred years ago between the Word and the Spirit. As a consequence of this split, there were churches that focused much of their time and attention on preaching the Word. They underscored the necessity of being born again and walking in holiness. Yet, they avoided topics about the power of the Holy Spirit in the supernatural and extraordinary miracles.

Likewise, there were churches that emphasized the supernatural power of the Holy Spirit to the exclusion of sound, biblical teaching. If we emphasize the Word without the Spirit, we will dry up. However, if we emphasize the Spirit without the Word, we will blow up. I don't think too many people would argue that we have witnessed churches dying on the vine because they've been without the Spirit, and there have been countless moral, ethical, and spiritual explosions within churches that lack character and sound biblical teaching on the subject of holiness. We need both, Word and Spirit, if we are going to accurately represent Jesus.

This subject can also be discussed utilizing the terms purity and power. Since the early 1900s, there have been many churches and denominations divided into these two camps. The challenge of my book and the topic of this chapter are to fuse purity and power (the Word and the Spirit). We have witnessed much progress in this fusion, but there is more that must transpire. This is such a vital topic and I pray that you will be deeply touched by what is discussed.

Rob: Dan, we often talk about the two-winged dove. You know that I devoted a lot of time on a dissertation defending the fusion of Word and Spirit or purity and power. I know this is an obvious question, but how essential is heart purity?

Dan: I don't believe that a person can sustain a Christian faith without experiencing and living the sanctified life. I believe that there are many people who experience the Holy Spirit when they are born again. They experience zeal and passion of that experience, but when God's Word draws us to this experience of being born again, it doesn't stop there. When we are born again, we get life, but the deeper call of the gospel is to give up our life. Unless we are willing to follow the Word of

God all the way to the cross and lay down our life we received from God, then that same Word that compelled us to Christ ends up being the same Word that condemns us. The Word of God stands against our carnal nature and it speaks to us about being crucified. And we'll always be in opposition to the Word until we come into total submission to God. I don't think that the supernatural lifestyle of the Spirit is sustainable without the character of Jesus, and we can't have the character of Jesus without experiencing the purification of the nature of our heart.

Rob: I know theoretically that God can regenerate you and purify you at the same time. So I don't ever want to put God in a box, but Dan, as I look at the Scripture and history of great saints, they seem to talk about a subsequent work after regeneration (being born again). Even in my own experience, I knew that I was sincerely born again—that my sins had been forgiven, but I later sensed a deeper call to heart purity. So as I said before, I don't ever want to put God in a box, but there seems to be a second, and sometimes a third or fourth work, that is subsequent to being born again. Can you talk about that?

Dan: What I have found has been interesting because when God first called me to this ministry,

He gave me a couple of mandates. The first mandate was to get prayer partners, but the second and main mandate was to live in the Bible. He instructed me to read through the Bible every month to learn the ministry and message of His Word. Each month when I would read the Bible, I would examine different themes. One month, I looked for all the verses that called us to be born again, adopted, justified, or to be "saved" from our sins. I found twenty-five verses that speak to that experience, but the next month God led me to look for verses that call us to holiness and sanctification. I believe at last count it was 600 plus verses.

Sanctification is both a work and a working. It usually follows after one is born again and in the family of God. What begins at a moment in time, the cleansing of your heart, becomes a lifetime of maturing in holiness. It is interesting how we can debate theology, but in all practicality you have to become a son before you can become an heir. There's a deeper work and blessing after a person has come into the family. I'm just thankful that He called me to this deep work and that I didn't have to understand it, but I just had to accept His Word in my life.

Rob: You know there is a lot of talk these days about progression or growing into sanctification. Talk about that because I typically believe it is both a "work and a working." To say it in similar ways, sanctification is an encounter and an encountering or a crisis experience and a continual experience. So it is not "either or," but rather it is "both and." Can you talk about that?

Dan: I think it is funny that we always get in these debates about crisis. I don't think it is a crisis, but rather I think it is a great experience. I don't think we should use the word "crisis," but I'm not a theologian—I'm a practitioner. There is a moment in time, though, when the nature of our life and the proneness of our heart are bent toward God instead of remaining on ourselves. I don't try to substantiate this with my ideas, but I always go back to the Word of God because it is the final authority. In the Scripture, I found different words that would describe this experience of heart purity happening within a moment.

First, the word baptism used by John the Baptist. He said that Jesus would come and baptize us with the Holy Spirit and fire in Luke 3:16. I don't believe baptism is classified as a process. I think when a person is baptized, they are instantly immersed and they know it. The same idea is true when one is baptized with the Holy Spirit.

Another word indicating a moment in time is circumcision. When Moses said in Deuteronomy 30:6 that we should circumcise our hearts and when Paul talked about a circumcision of the heart in Romans 2:29, I don't believe they were referring to a long process. I think someone would know if they are circumcised or not. I believe that God has the power to cut out of our heart and to circumcise the things that we were born with because of Adam's sin. The flesh and sin can be cut away through circumcision.

A third word that I found in the Bible is purge, such as in Isaiah 6:7 and John 15:2. Purged is a word that just simply means a supernatural work of God that eliminates all defilement from within. That is what happened with Isaiah when he was purged, and I don't think it was a process when the seraphim put the fiery coals on his mouth. I believe iniquity was burned out of him in a moment.

A fourth word that I found is cleanse. First John 1:9 says, "If we confess our sins, He is faithful and righteous to forgive us our sins and to cleanse us from all unrighteousness." I believe cleansing rids us of "all" unrighteousness. To cleanse means to sweep away all defilement, much like the word purge, and this cleansing occurs in a moment with the power of the Holy Spirit.

Another word that I came across while reading through the Psalms is the word create. David not only prayed that he would be forgiven, but he asked God to create a pure heart in him (Psalm 51:10). I love that. He prayed that God would *bara*, the Hebrew word for create, a new heart in him. Only God can create something and He can do so in a moment of time. He creates by merely speaking a word. Psalm 33:6 says, "By the word of the Lord the heavens were made . . ." God can create a pure heart with just a word.

The final word that I found indicating a moment in time is in Romans 6:8, 11. It's the word death. Paul told us to put this body of sin to death. I think we can be dying to different strongholds, different issues, and different things in our lives for a period of time, but I do believe that there is a moment when we are dead to sin. That is the moment that we cross through this door of having a heart that is divided between "us and God." This is the moment when we are dead to ourselves and when we are fully alive to Jesus only.

Rob: That is what Paul says in Galatians 2:20, "I have been crucified with Christ; and it is no longer I who live, but Christ lives in me; and the *life* which I now live in the flesh I live by faith in the Son of God, who loved me and gave Himself up for me." Listen to those words: I no longer live "but Christ lives in me." That's what you're talking about. We also read in James 1:8 about the double-minded person. James indicates that a double-minded man is unstable in all his ways. That instability has to stop. It has to come to an end. The answer comes in James 4:8 where he says, "Draw near to God and He will draw near to you. Cleanse your hands, you sinners; and purify your hearts, you double-minded." James is referring to a moment in time when this takes place.

You know, Dan, there's something helpful along these lines that J. A. Wood wrote about in the early 1900s. He discussed the difference between purity and maturity. I like to use the analogy of a marriage. I got married in 1985, and that was a moment in time. We weren't in the process of *getting* married—we were married. That was an instant moment in time, but Cindy and I have been growing and maturing in intimacy ever since that moment. Wood discussed the difference between purity and maturity, and I think that is where people get a little confused because purity can occur in a moment, but maturity is a lifetime process. The work of sanctification is both. Let me ask you, do you think sanctification is being taught?

Dan: In some places it is, but I don't believe it can be taught unless it has been experienced. What I have found in my travels is that people who are older than fifty years seem to talk about experiencing an Acts 2 moment where their hearts were purified. People younger than fifty years old can't seem to relate. I don't really know how to put my finger on it except that I never talked about sanctification until I had the experience myself. I don't believe you can lead someone into something that you don't possess yourself. I really can't answer if it is preached or not, but I know that I preach about it. I also know that to believe God can truly change our nature places a responsibility on us to actually walk in the sanctified life.

Rob: It is both, purity *and* power. I recently wrote a short booklet about that called, *The Fusion of Purity and Power.* But talk to us for a moment about the problem of having power with no purity because I believe that is a big problem, too. There are those who seem to underscore the supernatural power of the Holy Spirit without purity.

Dan: I like the analogy of the two-winged dove that we talk often about. One of the wings obviously is purity, but the other one is power. I believe if all we have is that power side, eventually we are going to blow up and become perverted. However, if all we have is the purity side, there is going to be no release of extraordinary power, and we are going to dry up and dissolve. So I think the danger of having power without purity is that we will eventually end up corrupting our ministries because that power will go to our head instead of continuing to flow out of a purified heart. I believe the only way to sustain a life of intimacy with Jesus is to have a pure heart, and it's the only way to function like Him, too.

Rob: Yes, I agree. Of course, there is a danger of purity without power, and isn't it true that when you started teaching that aspect of holiness, people thought you were teaching some new doctrine?

Dan: Well, I'm a Nazarene. My father–in–law, Don Owens, was a general superintendent in the Church of the Nazarene, and my daddy was a song evangelist in the Church of the Nazarene. My parents are saints. I'm fifty-four years old now and have been doing this enough to know there's a problem. During the first two and half

years of this calling, I preached on being sanctified—having a purified heart. When I preached
sanctification from that aspect, I was embraced
by everybody. I actually toured on forty different
districts. I was asked to speak at a national conference for the Church of the Nazarene, and it
was pretty amazing.

Yet, when the Lord started revealing to me that
He didn't want to just purify us and sanctify us
so that we would be holy enough to get to heaven
someday, but that His real purpose for sanctifying
us is so that we can be Christlike today and start
living and replicating this ongoing ministry of
Jesus, that is when conflict started for me. Jesus
said in John 14:12, "Truly, truly, I say to you, he
who believes in Me, the works that I do, he will
do also; and greater *works* than these he will do;
because I go to the Father." I actually believe that!

When I started preaching about the fact that God
doesn't just want us to become holy but that He
wants us to release His power, miraculous workings, healing, and deliverance through us as a
result of our holiness, I experienced push back
and uncertainty with people. What I found by
talking with a lot of my friends in leadership is
that many of the people in our Nazarene tribe
don't have a paradigm for the power and healing

side of the two-winged dove. We have never even approached that subject or been taught that it is possible, so that is what I have found in my journey so far. When I preach on just the half of the dove we are comfortable with, it is embraced, but when I start preaching on the whole dove, there is a little bit of nervousness in the crowds.

Rob: I experienced the same thing after my sabbatical. When I came back from my sabbatical in 2007, I was more interested in being a church with an atmosphere conducive to inhabit the manifest presence of God's glory. I had an encounter with His manifest presence in an overwhelming manner while I was on my sabbatical. I was forty-four, and I experienced something for the first time in my life.

Dan: Tell me about that, Rob. I want to hear about this experience you had on your sabbatical.

Rob: Well, like you I was reared in the Church of the Nazarene, so I embraced the message of heart purity, but I had never experienced the power of God. In 2007, I crawled out of my church. I was desperate, I was done, I was dry, and I had not heard the voice of God for at least two years. Our church was created around a "program." We had a Willow Creek type of service. We had people, we had programs, but we didn't have the presence. I didn't know what we lacked, but I just knew that we were in trouble.

When I left for my sabbatical, I was done with ministry as far as I was concerned. I didn't want to sin or do anything stupid, but I just didn't want to keep grinding on like I was. So I spent seven weeks on a sabbatical, and two of those weeks I spent in Summersville, West Virginia. It was during those two weeks that I was overcome, is the best way to describe it, by the manifest presence of God. We talk about the omnipresence of God which is everywhere, but the manifest presence is different.

John 14:21b says ". . . he who loves Me will be loved by My Father, and I will love him and will disclose Myself to him." Dan, I had never ever experienced that before that time. There were several days where I just lay on my back and these waves of God's glory just kept coming and coming. It was like in Isaiah 6, where Isaiah talks about the train of the robe filling the temple. Some expositors say "filling" is a present tense verb, and so God's presence kept filling, kept filling, and kept filling the temple. Well, that was what I felt.

I felt like there were waves of God's glory, and more waves, and more waves. I was undone. It just never stopped for three days. It was beyond being born again, beyond a consecration, and beyond sanctification. We might laugh in the Nazarene world, but it was like a third encounter, and it was a power encounter. I had never ever experienced anything like that awareness of His presence before.

When I came back from that experience, I had a renewed call to continue leading the church. And I told them that we would no longer design services for seekers, but we were going to build it for God's manifest presence. I wasn't concerned if people were happy with the service. I was more concerned if God was happy with our service. I desired for our services to be experiences like I had on my sabbatical. I wanted everyone to have an encounter. I believe anyone can experience God like I did. We instantly changed the paradigm of our church from being focused on people to being focused on His presence.

Dan: Stop, Rob! Stop! So you are talking about my passion now, but what I have found is that the more God reveals and releases His passion in my life the more division it causes in the body of Christ. Tell me about when you came back with this new vision, this new emphasis on your life for the glory of God to manifest. What did that do to your church?

Rob: Well, let me say that within one week it happened. The first Sunday after my sabbatical was unbelievable. I have been in the church all of my life, but I have never seen such an outpouring of God's glory. We saw people healed, delivered, set free, born again, and sanctified. We saw all of the nine supernatural gifts of 1 Corinthians 12 start to come alive in our church, and we will talk about this in a moment. Even though I didn't have a paradigm to even know what to call what was happening, I just knew that our services were being wrecked in the right way.

So, everyone seemed excited for a while, but this passion and pursuit of God didn't stop and neither did the manifestations of His presence. You mentioned the word "passion." When God does something that is not generated by the flesh but orchestrated by the Spirit, it is perpetuated. There were some in our church that thought all of this fervor and manifestations would die down— much like a pastor who comes back from a workshop but three months later everything goes back to normal and the zeal begins to wane. What was going on in our church, Dan, didn't stop. It only perpetuated.

We started having encounters with God. People would shout out during the middle of services, "Oh, my God, I just got healed," and no one touched them. People would come forward and say, "I think I got a word from God," and we didn't even know what to call it. They would have a specific word that someone would be healed, they would call that word out, and those people were healed specifically as they had heard. This continued for about three or four years and then we began to experience an exodus of people. We've had many people leave our church because they didn't like the idea of us pursuing the presence of God. And after I met Corey Jones, we felt led to change our midweek service to a prayer service. We started crying out on Wednesdays for *more* of His presence. I remember a letter that I received that stated, "This church prays too much." More people left because not everyone desired to pursue the presence of God or steward a revival culture with humility, passion, and hunger.

I guess I would say to any pastor or leader that there is a price to pay for pressing into God. Not everyone is going to run after the manifest presence of God's glory. I say it this way: His presence is attractive to some but repulsive to others. When the glory fell in our church, it was exciting and it was delineating. There were those who did not push into God's presence. We never compromised the message either. We were still preaching the message of purity and calling people to consecration. We were calling people to die to themselves, but simultaneously to preaching the message of holiness we experienced works, miracles, and supernatural occurrences that I had never seen in my entire life. The power of God came down, Dan, and it was remarkable to say the least.

Dan: Who did you share your experiences with? Who did you have that was like a brother in arms or a mentor you could share these experiences with?

Rob: I had one guy, Kevin Seymour, who has been my friend for over thirty years. He was the only other one I shared with — only he hadn't had his encounter yet. His encounter came later for him, and when it did, he experienced an exodus from his church, too. However, before his encounter with God, I remember going out to lunch with him and sharing some of our experiences with him, and he just looked across the table at me.

Outside of Kevin, I shared with no one — at least within the Church of the Nazarene.

I felt like I had to fly beneath the radar. I didn't know you, I didn't know Corey Jones, and I didn't know others in our denomination that had these kinds of encounters. Here is the disturbing fact, Dan, there wasn't a paradigm to know how to operate in this kind of outpouring. I have completed college and seminary in our Nazarene institutions. I'm not trying to make a cheap shot toward our schools, but I'm just telling you that we don't teach or train our leaders how to function in this kind of supernatural lifestyle.

Therefore, I did not have a paradigm when all of this started happening. I went a year or so looking for answers. Obviously, I turned to the Word. I consumed the Word to find answers to what was happening. The Scripture was *breathed* into existence. Second Timothy 3:16, "All Scripture is inspired by God and profitable for teaching, for reproof, for correction, for training in righteousness." I found my answers in God's Word. Other than the Bible, I had to go outside of our tribe to get language for what was happening.

Dan: It is time for that to end! We are a holiness denomination with a picture on our church signs of a dove coming down and kissing a Bible. We probably ought to make that our reality and not just a sign.

Rob: Yes! Dan, we were birthed in this—in purity and power. My dissertation focused on our denomination, the Church of the Nazarene. The Holiness movement, which includes the Pentecostals, Charismatics, Nazarenes, Wesleyans, and many others too, all came out of that stream of purity and power. It was both aspects. So, we must embrace both purity and power. It is the infusion of both and not the exclusion of either. You have already alluded to this, but Word churches that only emphasize purity will dry up, and power churches who only emphasize the Spirit will blow up. We need the integration of both, Dan, and I'm praying and believing that across our tribe and others like ours, we will embrace purity and power.

Dan: I think ultimately that our pursuit, our purity, our passion, and our power are all about Jesus. When we study the Scripture, for instance, the message that Peter preached right out of His encounter of the baptism of the Holy Spirit in Acts 2 . . . his message was split right down the middle between the prophetic wing of power, quoting Joel, and the holiness wing of the Word, quoting David. Right in the middle are these three little verses about Jesus who came demonstrating miracles, signs, and wonders, and then died, was buried, and rose from the dead.

Jesus is the heart of what we are talking about—He is the life. To be sanctified is to be "Christified" if you will. We look exactly like Him. In this lifetime, our call is to become like He was. Jesus flowed in holiness of character, morality, and compassion, but He also flowed in power, wonders, signs, and gifts. He is our example of what it is to be a sanctified Christian. Jesus is our template. He is our pattern.

Rob: That is true. I'm not chasing one wing or the other, but I desire to be just like Him. Luke 6:40a says, ". . . but everyone, after he has been fully trained, will be like his teacher." We will be just like Jesus. He was character, and He was charismata. He was the epitome of both wings. So, if we are just like Him, both wings will be evident in our lives.

Dan: Amen!

There are several observations I have drawn from this interview with Dan. First, I believe that it is incorrect to define sanctification in terms of being set apart *from* something without talking about being set apart *for* something. Sanctification is more than "being good" and avoiding sin. Sanctification means that we have been set apart and ordained for a spiritual priesthood. A priest was someone who ideally inquired of the Lord to discharge God's mandates, God's prophetic Word, and God's assignments to His people. My friend and mentor, Jon Ruthven, wrote me an e-mail concerning this subject matter. Listen to what he wrote:

> When a priest functions prophetically, they are involved in healing. So, if you are sanctified or made holy in the biblical sense, you will be commissioned, set apart, and sanctified by God to replicate the ministry of Jesus and introduce the kingdom of God and the Spirit of God in charismatic power. The real gospel will be the miracle power (*dunamis*) of God unto salvation, which will include healing, deliverance, and preservation—not just getting people ready for heaven.

By using the word "charismatic," we are talking about being empowered by God's grace. There is no gospel without grace, and there certainly is no spiritual walk without grace. Grace is a divine force that operates through God's people. Anyone who is sanctified will function in this divine force, power, and grace. Therefore, when sanctified, we will replicate Jesus not just in terms of morality and character, but we will replicate Him in the nature of His power, signs, and miracles. Ruthven concluded his e–mail to me with these words,

> Sanctification implies a relationship with God where believers are led by the Spirit, actually fulfilling the holy functions of the priesthood with behavior, which rightly reflects the power of the Holy Spirit.

There is no question that purity and power are cooperative and evident in a sanctified believer. The problem is, however, we have held tightly to a form of godliness while denying the power (2 Timothy 3:5). We have pushed away from power, God's *dunamis* anointing that enables us to function charismatically, and we have accepted a lifeless form of holiness. In reality, I don't believe we can call ourselves "sanctified." Like the unbelieving Sadducees in Matthew 22:29, many of us in holiness churches don't know the Scripture or the power of God's Spirit. We need a fresh baptism with the Holy Spirit that will not merely set us apart from sin and iniquity, but will ignite us with a holy fervor that will be demonstrated with supernatural power, signs, and wonders.

Second, if we attempt to function in the power of the Holy Spirit, then we might as well accept the fact that there will always be pushback from people not interested, too fearful, or too filled with unbelief. It's not a matter of "if" you will receive criticism but a matter of "when." I'm not suggesting that we should intentionally stir up conflict or engage in hostile debates, but when you start functioning in extraordinary power, religious spirits will combat you. Jesus healed a man who was crippled. He was unable to function normally and quite possibly his ability to provide for his family was impaired as well. His withered hand probably was a social embarrassment for him, but in a matter of moments, Jesus healed this guy and everything changed for the good. You would think that this demonstration of power would have given cause for celebration and praise to God. However, it was not met with applause but rather disdain. The Bible indicates that the religious group plotted how they might destroy Jesus on account of it (Matthew 12:14).

Had Jesus merely fed the hungry crowds and clothed naked people, He would have been accepted by the mainstream religious party. But the fact that He operated in charismatic power and claimed to be one with the Father was too much for them to swallow. His demonstrations of extraordinary power offended people and caused them to be indignant toward Christ. It will be no different for anyone reading this book. The moment you start functioning in the power of the Holy Spirit and claim to be one with the Father (see John 17:21), you will be labeled, branded, and criticized. Religious spirits will do everything possible to dumb down the release of God's Holy Spirit through your life. You can talk about being sanctified and ready for heaven one day, but should you talk about laying hands on the sick, casting out demons, healing diseased and crippled people, or raising the dead — the very activities that we were commissioned to do (Matthew 10:8) — you will be in for a battle.

For several years there has been considerable talk about "strange fire" coming into the church. Our *real* problem is "no fire." We started out in the Spirit many years ago, but too many of us have reverted to the flesh (Galatians 3:3). We talk about *our* programs, *our* ministries, *our* services, *our* churches, and *our* small groups, but there is little talk about the extraordinary outpouring of the Holy Spirit. We are not being overwhelmed with stories of healing, deliverance, and citywide spiritual transformation.

Paul warned us, "Do not quench the Spirit; do not despise prophetic utterances" (1 Thessalonians 5:19–20). This is a command to not put the fire of God out. He's telling us to not place a blanket over the Holy Spirit's fire. Additionally, Paul told us to not treat prophecy, which is the inspirational unction of the Holy Spirit, with contempt. Where are the prophetic voices in our churches? Why are we told to seek after the gift of prophecy, but there is little seeking for it on our churches (1 Corinthians 14:1)? There can be no other conclusion than we are snuffing out the work of the Spirit in favor of our own human cleverness.

I cannot begin to tell you how many pastors (usually within the Church of the Nazarene) share the same lament with me, and it's the same story over and over. They became desperate and hungry for more of God. They eventually experienced an encounter with His manifest presence, and when God's glory fell on their churches, they experienced opposition from leaders in their churches or from their districts. Our churches in America are declining. We are in financial trouble, and it's only being eclipsed by our spiritual decline. We *need* a fresh outpouring of the Holy Spirit! We need a sweeping move of God that will wreck our "status quo."

You have to decide if you desire His presence more than you desire acceptance from the religious majority. Please, make no mistake about this: if you press into the manifest presence of God and experience encounters with the Holy Spirit, you will be challenged by the enemy on every front. Religious spirits will arise through persecution, through carnal self–centered people, and through "unbelieving believers" in your church, denominations, and among your peers. Jesus was even thought to be crazy among His own family (Mark 3:21). It just might be the same for you if you function in the presence and power of the Holy Spirit.

My third observation has to do with the Christian educational system so prominent in our Western culture. What I find so disheartening is that I, and many others like me, have been poorly trained in the kinds of activities that Jesus trained His followers in. When Jesus deployed His disciples, He gave them instructions about preaching the kingdom and healing the sick. He imparted an authority upon them so they could overcome demonic obstacles. Later, He imparted the Holy Spirit and power that enabled them to do the same works as He did and to even exceed Him (John 14:12).

Our Christian educational process awards diplomas to students who then enter into churches with no knowledge about the charismatic power of the Holy Spirit. Sixty-five percent of the words in the gospel of Mark describing Jesus' public ministry were about supernatural acts of power. Yet the educational process in our Christian colleges and seminaries rarely talk about the supernatural activities of Jesus. What are students being prepared to do? I certainly have no problem with teaching young people a myriad of subjects in their Christian education, but where are the classes about speaking prophetically over our cities? Where are the classes about intercessory prayer, desperation for the presence of God, fasting, and crying out for fresh encounters with God? Where are the classes about the supernatural gifts in 1 Corinthians 12 that should manifest through Spirit–filled believers?

What I find even more disheartening is that these charismatic activities are often denigrated in the "educated" mind. We have elevated academics over the anointing. We prefer to promote someone to a prominent position of leadership based on the degrees behind their name or from the accolades in the wake of their success. It's a good thing that we weren't electing the positions in the New Testament Church because we would have missed the characteristics they looked for.

The early church looked for people with a good reputation and those filled with the Holy Spirit and with wisdom (Acts 6:3). Two of the lay leaders chosen, Stephen and Philip, operated in power, wonders, signs, and miracles (Acts 6:8; 8:6–7). Why wouldn't we consider someone to lead a church with those same qualifications? What if we honored the anointing more than anything else? I have nothing against being fully trained in a Bible college or seminary. I have spent many hours, and many dollars, pursuing a formal education, yet I heard precious little that prepared me and trained me to operate in the manifest power of the Holy Spirit.

I'm simply suggesting that we make room for the activity of the Holy Spirit. Let's begin to expose students in our Christian colleges to the supernatural activities of the Spirit. Let's send them to a Dan Bohi crusade or to a prayer conference in Texas led by Pastor Corey Jones. Let's pause for fifteen minutes in our college classrooms before we dismiss a group of students and invite the Holy Spirit to manifest Himself upon the students. Let's spend some time in our classes listening to the guidance, prompting, and prophetic utterances of the Holy Spirit. Let's talk about the extraordinary power of the Holy Spirit and do so without downplaying His miracles or questioning the validity of the Bible. Let's help our students enter the ministry with both wings. Let's help them function like Jesus did in purity and power.

Chapter Three

MIRACLE STORIES

Paul wrote in Romans 1:16, "For I am not ashamed of the gospel, for it is the power of God for salvation . . ." Salvation is the Greek word *soteria*, which means deliverance, healing, and restoration. This word not only refers to a moral and spiritual restoration, but a physical and mental regeneration. Physical and emotional healing always accompanied the gospel message in the New Testament. Jesus didn't merely "pray a sinner's prayer" with people, He healed their bodies. When Philip entered Samaria, his message to these people included miracles and signs (Acts 8:5–7). When Paul and Barnabas shared stories about their ministry among the Gentiles, those stories included signs and wonders (Acts 15:12).

Healing and deliverance are part of the package. You cannot cut and chop those elements from the gospel message in favor of only getting one's sins cleansed. I realize that having our hearts cleansed from sin and its power is essential to enter into eternal life; however, I'm simply saying that we don't need to exclude the *full* gospel message of its power to bring salvation to every area of our lives.

The power from God for miracles and wonders are actually "signs" of believing in and following Jesus. Jesus said, "These signs will accompany those who have believed. . . ." (Mark 16:17). After stating that, Jesus identified four signs in particular. I believe that there are *many* signs, but in this passage Jesus identified four. The word sign (*semeion*) means a distinguishing mark that authenticates something. It indicates if something is genuine or real. If a legal document was stamped with a sign, that sign indicated the authenticity of the document. Signs that follow believers indicate that they are *real* followers of Jesus. They are confirmation. That is why Mark 16:20 says, ". . . the Lord worked with them, and confirmed the word by the signs that followed."

Look closely at this verse in Mark 16:17. We are *not* chasing after signs. Our focus is Jesus. These are signs that "accompany" those who have put their faith in Christ and are walking in intimacy with Him. In other words, if we follow Christ, then signs will follow us. The signs merely point to a greater reality — namely Jesus. A sign that says "fire extinguisher" points to a greater reality, which is the actual fire extinguisher. The same is true with signs that accompany a believer. They always point to Jesus. What accompanies us should always point to Him. If we are filled with the Holy Spirit and walking in intimacy with Jesus, then our lives will give evidence to that fact. There will be signs that point to that reality. We will manifest spiritual fruit (Galatians 5:22–23) and spiritual functions (1 Corinthians 12:8–10). Our lives will produce character and *charismata* (spiritual gifts). Most people don't think twice about spiritual fruit, but they tend to get nervous when we address supernatural spiritual gifts being the byproduct of a Spirit–filled life. But these extraordinary gifts, wonders, and signs were evident in the life of Jesus and His followers in the book of Acts.

This chapter focuses on the miracles that have accompanied Dan's ministry. We will begin with people who have been physically touched and healed. I have personally witnessed many unforgettable miracles while traveling with him. I don't believe that he set out to become a "healing" minister, but he does believe the gospel will bring healing. Every miracle and every healing points people to Jesus, never to Dan. So when you read the stories we discussed in our interview, please understand that *we* are not the healers.

That being said, Jesus longs to use people. He deeply desires to pour His power through us so that needy, broken, diseased, and crippled people may know the love of God. He wants the world to know that God so loves them and that He has the power to touch them physically, emotionally, and spiritually. If we will remain surrendered to Jesus and if we will continue to walk in the Spirit, we will become instruments that God can use in supernatural ways.

Rob: Dan, I want to talk about miracle stories. I have read about miracles in history and we read about them in the Word of God, but I had never encountered the kinds of miracles that we experienced the first year after my sabbatical. I have seen blind eyes opened, people get out of wheelchairs, instantaneous healings and deliverances, deaf ears healed, backs and knees healed, and a host of spiritual miracles. It's interesting that the first year after my sabbatical we saw more people born again than in the nine years before by trying to run slick programs. I believe it was the sheer presence of God drawing people to Him.

I want to talk with you about transforming miracles because there is no way that we can avoid the kinds of things you have seen. You certainly don't chase after miracles, yet they are the result of the manifest presence of God and obviously the result of what is happening in and through you. Talk about when you began to see the increase of miracles in your ministry and share some of the more significant ones. I know we could talk the rest of the day on this, but which ones really stick out in your mind?

Dan: It's hard to hone in on which ones to pick, but there have been many occasions now where people who have been wheelchair bound with diseases, such as MS or Lou Gehrig's disease, have been touched by God. They were able to get up and walk with balance and strength.

There have been many occasions where cancer has disappeared within a number of hours after praying. I remember the time when a lady came to a service in North Dakota. She had a lump on her breast so we prayed, and a day and a half later she went to the doctor who reported that the cancer was gone.

The miraculous power of God is real, but it is hard to figure out because sometimes it is more prevalent in some services than at other times. I believe that the more I study the Scripture and the more I try to practice the life and ministry of Jesus—if I try to separate the Word from the miraculous, I have totally dismantled the point of the gospel. I feel like if we are really preaching the Word in the anointing, that the hand of God, which is referred to as the power of God in the book of Acts, is always present *with* the Word. I believe the miracles just happen as long as we don't compromise on the Word. I don't think we can separate the Word and the Spirit. In fact, I think the reason that we have to even talk about two wings is evidence that the Church has fallen from its original mandate to go and make disciples in the authority we were given.

The Church originally didn't worry if it was purity or power. The early believers just lived the life of Jesus. Jesus told us in Matthew 10 that we should heal the sick, raise the dead, cast out demons, cleanse the lepers, and preach the kingdom. He says that if we have freely received, we will freely give. I think it is hard for some people who don't want to receive the reality of the kingdom in power to actually give it away. I think there has to be a receiving before there can be a giving. There are a lot of well–meaning, sanctified believers who have actually received the purity and the holiness of God, but they haven't received the reality of the kingdom of God in terms of power.

Until we come full circle back to Acts being the genesis of the Church and not the revelation of the Church, the realization of power is going to be hit and miss. We must realize that Acts is supposed to be the start of the Church, and we should be beyond it by now. My prayer and desire is that this awakening that God is calling us to will unite more and more people and that we will be brought into the stream of God's power, miraculous wonders, and His workings to the point that it won't be a discussion any more, but rather it will just be part of our everyday, ongoing life.

Rob: It is interesting that Paul wrote in Romans 1:16 how he wasn't ashamed of the gospel because it had power to bring salvation. Isn't it true that "salvation" encompasses healing, deliverance, and restoration?

Dan: Absolutely!

Rob: So to delineate salvation from healing or from deliverance should not be done because it's a package deal, and you really can't separate it into individual parts. I realize this question arouses much controversy, but Jesus never really commanded us to pray for the sick, did He?

Dan: Not in the gospels. He commanded the disciples on numerous occasions to *heal* the sick but not to pray for the sick. He even commanded the seventy-two to heal the sick and to preach the kingdom. The closest place where we're commanded to pray for the sick is in James. He wrote, "Is anyone among you sick? Then he must call for the elders of the church and they are to pray over him, anointing him with oil in the name of the Lord; and the prayer offered in faith will restore the one who is sick. . . ." (James 5:14–15). But Jesus never commanded people to pray for the sick.

However, I pray for people everywhere I go because I don't think that I am to the level where I should be. If I really was going to take Jesus seriously, I would just operate in His authority. My goal someday is to get to the place where I can just walk into the room, and God will do the healing because I stepped in with His presence on me. That is my goal, Rob.

Rob: Yes! The Bible says, "I do not possess silver and gold, but what I do have I give to you: In the name of Jesus Christ the Nazarene — walk" (Acts 3:6). We have Him! Let's give Him away. This opens the conversation to living in the supernatural. You know that I wrote a workbook about the supernatural gifts in 1 Corinthians 12. You have read that and you have heard me teach on that subject, but this all just came alive for you, didn't it? The supernatural gifts just seemed to explode through you.

Dan: They really did, Rob. You know it is interesting, back in 2010, about a year into my ministry of this awakening, I was touring in Texas for one month. I was in all three of the Texas districts. During my first district tour with Dr. Duane Srader, I was in a church in Orange, Texas, and I was just starting to preach. All of a sudden, about five minutes into my message, I saw this lid come in over the church, and I didn't know what to think about it.

God gave me a vision of a lid that prevented His glory from entering in. The lid had something to do with the fact that there was no desperation or repentance. I tried to ignore it, but I couldn't. It didn't go away. It was strange because it was right then that I realized that I had a choice to make. I could follow the leading of the Holy Spirit and pronounce that there was a lid — nothing was going to happen with this lid anyways, or I could compromise and just try to do a church service. Through fear I said, "I don't think we need to continue the service because I don't believe anyone here is desperate."

When I said that it was very quiet, even scary, and I was shaking, but as I look back on it I know that it was discerning the spirits, the gift of faith, a prophetic utterance, and a word of knowledge all working in me, but I didn't have a paradigm for it then because I never was taught about the power side of the dove. As I said before, I was reared learning about the purity side of the dove. Anyways, I remember that after making that announcement, we all waited in silence, but I was hoping something would happen because I felt embarrassed. I even felt fearful. Then, in a moment or so, a lady stood up and said, "It is my fault, I didn't pray about the songs that I sang," and she came to the altar followed by two hundred more people. One courageous lady repented publically, and then the rest of the church followed.

Dr. Srader put on his praise report the next day that two hundred people were touched because of one woman. I knew something had happened that evening because, when people got up from the altar, their faces were shining and the lid was gone. I learned such a lesson that day from the Holy Spirit. When there is corporate repentance, we can receive a corporate anointing. Every believer has the Spirit of God in them. Jesus lives inside of each of us. I believe He is the gate of heaven, so everything that comes from the heavenly realms comes through Jesus, the gate, into our realm. Think about it this way: there are little open heavens above us, and everywhere we go the kingdom of God can flow through us.

Rob: Amen. That is so good.

Dan: Listen, if everyone in a church repents and everyone is unified around the manifest presence of Jesus, it makes that gate bigger over all of us. I believe this ushers in a corporate anointing and greater things can be accomplished. Think about Acts chapter 2. They *all* had the fire of God's Spirit on them—not just 40 or 50 percent. It was the first time in the history of the world that all of God's people were filled with the Holy Spirit. As a result, amazing things began to happen on the day of Pentecost.

Rob: Yes, yes! I agree.

Dan: So that night in Orange, Texas, the lid was removed, and the Spirit was able to work with power. When the people went back to their seats, the Lord spoke to me, "I want you to go pray for this young lady." I didn't know exactly how to do it, but I went over to her and asked if she was in pain. She said, "Yes," and I prayed for her. She fell down on the ground. I didn't know what to think or what it meant, but when she got up she had no pain.

Then she touched the lady next to her and that lady started crying because her back was healed, and then the lady whose back was healed touched the man behind her and his marriage was healed, and that man touched Dr. Srader and he started laying hands on the person next to him, and before I knew it, the whole church was just laying hands on each other, praying for one another, crying, and blessing one another.

While all of this was happening, I looked across the room and saw this young man. The Lord gave me a picture of four arrows in the back of his heart. That might sound like the dumbest thing you've heard, but I know now that it was a word of knowledge and a prophetic picture. I didn't understand it then because, as I said, I didn't have a paradigm for these things. I walked over to him and said, "I want to pray for you, sir." I told him that I felt like he had four arrows in his heart, and they were sticking through his back. He said, "Well, as a matter of fact, forty people left my church two weeks ago, and they are all talking behind my back. I'm so discouraged, but when you told me about these arrows, it gave me hope again."

I had no idea at the time how all of this could work. After that service, I went out to eat with Dr. Srader and we couldn't believe all that God had done that night. The next night, we were in Lake Houston, Texas, and I was preaching on sanctification. Several hundred people came forward to be sanctified. That same night I had a word of knowledge of twenty-six people being healed of depression, and exactly twenty-six people came running forward and we prayed over them—all of them were healed. I found out two years later while in Conro, Texas, that the twenty-sixth person to be healed that night in Lake Houston was the piano player. She had manic-depressive illness her whole life, and that night she was totally set free.

Rob: Praise God!

Dan: I believe in this, Rob! Anyways, that night in Lake Houston, at the conclusion of the service and as I was getting ready to leave, there was a lady on the front row. I walked up to her because I felt like I was supposed to pray for her, and she looked at me and said, "I knew you were going to pray for me, Dan." I said, "How did you know that?" She proceeded to tell me that the lady that I prayed for in Orange, Texas, who fell down after I prayed for her, was her daughter. She told me that her daughter had struggled with fibromyalgia for two years and she had trouble sleeping at night, but after I had prayed for her, she was able to sleep all night.

The next morning she called her mother and said that God had healed her, and then she said to her mother, "If you have Dan touch you, you can be healed, too." This mother was so energized with faith because her daughter had passed on the gift of faith to her over the phone. I had no clue what had taken place in the Spirit.

I think that when the Spirit gets flowing in and through us, we can touch people and give to others around us what the Spirit is doing inside us. We are giving away the Spirit "one to another," and this is normal Christianity. So I prayed for that lady, and I finished the tour with Dr. Srader. In my next assignment I spent ten days with Dr. Jones on the West Texas district tour. About ten days after that night in Lake Houston, I got a call from that lady on the front row that knew I was going to pray for her (whose daughter got healed of fibromyalgia). I will never forget her words, I was almost in shock. She said, "Brother Dan, that night when you prayed with me, I was healed. I have had lupus and fibromyalgia for eighteen years and have struggled with pain, but for the last ten days I have been running every day because I don't have any pain, and I wanted you to know."

That is when it started to dawn on me that the power of the Spirit is real if we will just walk in the impressions God puts on our hearts. He can do the miraculous because He hasn't changed. We are the ones who limit God sometimes. I don't claim to have a great knowledge of all this stuff, but I feel like I'm an apprentice who is learning. Those nine functions in 1 Corinthians 12:8–10 work together, and if we will stay in intimacy with Jesus and in the simplicity of faith, the impulses that God has in His heart have to be released through us. We can be those people who carry His heart, His passion, and His power to those around us. I'm really excited about what God started to show me back in 2010, and it has just intensified since then.

Rob: We have to stay in the posture of a learner. We need to remain teachable. I didn't have the language for it when it started happening in my church and ministry. I have language for it now, but that certainly doesn't make me an expert in this. One thing that I have learned, and it is a paradigm shift for some people, is if I have the Holy Spirit in me, then I am going to grow in *all* of the fruit and I'm going to be a potential candidate to function in *all* of the supernatural gifts (*charismata*) in 1 Corinthians 12.

In other words, I was taught that I was given *one* gift, and that's all I had. However, when you look at 1 Corinthians 12, it's not about the gift you have, but it's about the Holy Spirit who has you. This passage is not about us wielding our gift, but rather it is about the Holy Spirit who has possessed us and how He chooses to flow through us. He is on display, in other words, and we are the instrument He uses.

What you just described here, Dan, from your time in Texas, brings to mind an analogy I talk about when I teach on the supernatural gifts. I have a 125-foot garden hose that reaches out to my garden. At the end of that hose, I have a nozzle, and if I want a different application of water, then I just click it for a different flow. It is the same water, but I can choose mist, spray, shower, jet, or soak. I just stand there and click the nozzle, and it takes that water and applies it in a different way. What you are talking about, Dan, relates to how I see the Holy Spirit desiring to flow through us anyway that He desires — some might be in a mist, others might be a jet flow, but it changes according to the Holy Spirit.

We're describing a lifestyle not just for you, Dan, but for all of us if we are in the Spirit. This isn't just for certain people. This is life in the Spirit for every single person. I know that the supernatural is not something we chase. In fact, it says in Mark 16:17, "These signs will accompany those who have believed." Therefore, we follow Him, we are in Him, and these signs just follow after us, and it is just the natural outpouring of being in the Spirit and walking intimately with Jesus.

I want to return to something that you mentioned earlier, words of knowledge. That first year when the manifest presence of God began to show up in our church, we prayed for a spirit of wisdom and revelation (see Ephesians 1:17). Revelation means to just lift the veil. Well, the veil was lifted, and we saw things in the Spirit we had never seen before. Paul said in 1 Corinthians 14:1, "Pursue love, yet desire earnestly spiritual *gifts*, but especially that you may prophesy." Let me demystify prophecy: it is just hearing the Lord speak. The Bible says, "My sheep hear My voice, and I know them, and they follow Me" (John 10:27).

We all hear His voice, or we wouldn't be born again. So, if we can hear His voice, then we can speak what He is saying, and that is speaking prophetically. Prophecy is speaking what God is saying to us about someone or something. But with that prophetic ability — the ability to hear God speak — comes these "words of knowledge." A word of knowledge is one of the manifestations mentioned in 1 Corinthians 12. Talk to me about that . . . about how words of knowledge specifically work. What are they? How have you seen them in operation?

Dan: Well, one time I was in Missouri at a seven church gathering, and while I was preaching, the Lord specifically told me that someone was being healed on the left side of the sanctuary. I obviously didn't have a paradigm for what that meant because I wasn't taught that functioning in the nine gifts of the Holy Spirit was normal Christianity, and so I didn't know how to deal with it. I tried to ignore it, but for about five minutes it was like I didn't know how to speak anymore because God had silenced my voice. So I said, "I don't know what this means, but I feel like someone over here is being healed. I should have said it five minutes ago, but I was afraid to say it."

At that moment a lady stood up, and she said, "Brother Dan, while I was on a work and witness trip, I fell and hurt my arm. I've had nerve damage in my arm ever since then and was scheduled for surgery. About five minutes ago I felt a warm tingling in my arm, and there is no pain." She was waving her arm and crying, and all of a sudden people started running to the altar. It was really weird and awesome at the same time. I got a letter from Steve Profit, the pastor who was organizing the gathering that night, and in the letter he wrote that a couple hundred people were sanctified, seventy people gave their life to Jesus and were born again, and there were thirty-seven miracles of healing.

This brings me to this amazing concept that I have come to realize in 1 Corinthians 12:7 where it says, "But to each one is given the manifestation of the Spirit for the common good." When the release of one of these gifts comes out of us, like you described about the nozzle on the end of the hose, it benefits everyone. When I had a word of knowledge about someone being healed, it wasn't just for her. It touched her and many other people were benefited with purification, deliverance, and healing. God gave me information—knowledge—about someone, and hundreds benefited from that knowledge. I have seen that over and over again.

At a meeting in Nampa, Idaho, I had a word of knowledge for someone's deaf ear that needed to be healed. All of a sudden this lady stood up crying, and she came forward and wanted to testify. She said that she was a minister of intercession and a high school teacher, but she was deaf in her ear. However, when I spoke those words, that someone's ear needed healed, she said that she felt warm air blowing in her ear. She said, "I didn't think anything at all could happen because I didn't come to an altar, but all of a sudden I just started calling people on the phone and could actually hear them."

Her testimony spurred on all kinds of other people who came running to the altar there at Nampa First Church of the Nazarene. I believe when the functions of the precious Holy Spirit are released through us, it doesn't just affect the person in front of us, but it flows to everyone around them. And the repercussions of the Spirit's influence should never end as long as we don't stop pursuing intimacy with Jesus.

I'm excited about words of knowledge. I have now seen hundreds and hundreds of people touched through this particular manifestation of the Spirit. I have spoken words of knowledge to people, and it has touched them so deeply that they have blessed me with huge financial contributions to our ministry—just from one word of knowledge. I hate to admit this, but one time someone was so transformed by a word of knowledge that they gave our ministry a $70,000 gift. It has nothing to do with money, but it's about the power of the Spirit touching people's lives. We shouldn't be ashamed to speak God's words to people because we have no idea what God is trying to do with His Word when it's being released unto the earth.

Rob: What exactly are words of knowledge?

Dan: I believe words of knowledge are just that: "knowledge" about someone or something. This is knowledge that you can only know through God's revelation. Sometimes God will send a solution to someone's situation. The point is that God uses this knowledge to touch people. There are many people who love God. They study His Word, but sometimes God uses other people in His body to bring healing and restoration to the body. Words of knowledge are some of the most tangible ways to receive healing. It's the body healing the body. There is a lot of controversy over this because some people think that a word of knowledge can be manipulation. But from my experience, I haven't seen people hurt by words of knowledge. I have seen people healed and delivered because of them. I believe in words of knowledge.

Rob: Look at Jesus in John 4:16, "Go, call your husband and come here." Jesus knew this woman's situation. He had a word of knowledge about her many husbands. The end result of Jesus' word of knowledge was that this woman returned to Samaria, and the Bible says in John 4:39, "From that city many of the Samaritans believed in Him because of the word of the woman who testified, 'He told me all the things that I have done'." Imagine an entire city turned around and touched because of words of knowledge!

Dan: They are to be used for the profit of all (see 1 Corinthians 12:7).

Rob: What is most interesting in the life of the supernatural is that these words of knowledge we're talking about are not reserved for inside the walls of the church. Many times you have been seated at restaurants and a waitress or waiter comes up, and Jesus begins to download some information into your heart about them. The end result is that they open their heart up to Jesus. I was sitting with my friend, Chad Cline, at Red Robin, and the waiter came and Chad said, "I feel like you are going through some very difficult things in your life right now." The guy came to the table and spent a few minutes as Chad spoke into his heart with words of knowledge. Within a few minutes, this guy gave his life to Jesus and made a profession of faith. That is the profit of all, and it can even happen outside the walls of the church.

Dan: Amen.

As we conclude this chapter, I feel compelled to talk about the necessity of listening to the gentle whispers of the Holy Spirit. Dan spoke about the Holy Spirit speaking to him on several different occasions, and while he heard the Spirit speaking to him, it required him stepping out of the ordinary and comfortable box to obey. My challenge to those reading this is that we must learn to obey the Holy Spirit even when it seems odd or different from the order of things we're used to.

The mistake we often make is to stay locked into our Sunday morning programs and service formats and miss what the Holy Spirit desires to do. There is nothing wrong with an order of service, but we should hold them loosely. I realize that God can give us direction long before a service begins, and we will follow that program just as He inspired. However, we should never be so concerned about our agenda that we miss those instantaneous moments when the Holy Spirit desires to lead us in a different direction.

I was reading about Jim Cymbala, pastor of Brooklyn Tabernacle, speaking at a large church. He said that just before the service the entire worship team gathered in the green room to go over the service that was about to begin. Everything was timed down to the minute. The worship leader actually told someone to trim their prayer down to allow more time for the offering. Pastor Cymbala was told exactly how long to preach and that he wouldn't be able to pray at the end of the message because of a special music number the choir was singing. What struck Cymbala the most, besides the tightly wound schedule, was the prayer that was offered before they left the green room to start the service. The guy said, "Oh, Spirit of God, come and move among us with blessing and power. Have your way as we yield ourselves to you."[1]

Were these people *really* expecting or anticipating the Holy Spirit to come with blessing and power? And what if He actually tried to move in? Cymbala said that there was a meeting that night, but not too many people had a meeting with God.[2] I fear that too many of us have become accustomed to our old wine skins (see Luke 5:37–39). We have become too attached to our paradigms. The Holy Spirit deeply desires to manifest Himself for the profit of all. He desires to pour out upon His people. He desires to heal, restore, redeem, deliver, and touch His people. The question is, "Are we leaning into His Spirit to hear Him?" And should He speak to us, are we willing to follow His leading even if it doesn't make sense at the moment? Let me say again, there is nothing wrong with our "order of service." But we cannot be so tightly programmed that we miss those moments when the Holy Spirit interrupts with a divine agenda.

The fact is I believe that all of us can hear these "interruptions" if we're sensitive to the Holy Spirit. Additionally, I believe that we can all hear words of knowledge as Dan discussed. The reason is I believe that the Holy Spirit desires to use every person in extraordinary ways. The supernatural lifestyle should become the natural lifestyle for all Spirit–filled believers. We often treat miracles, signs, and wonders as "once in a lifetime" occurrences when I believe they are part of walking in the Spirit. Peter said that when the Holy Spirit is poured out in the last days, everyone will prophesy (Acts 2:17).

Everyone can hear the Holy Spirit and everyone can speak His words. This *is* the New Covenant that Isaiah wrote about. He wrote about a day when God would put His Spirit on all people and place His words in our mouth (Isaiah 59:21). This promise was fulfilled at Pentecost when the Spirit was poured out, and it is fulfilled through prophetic words of knowledge when God speaks to us about people, situations, or circumstances. This is why we must live with our ears inclined to the Lord (Isaiah 55:3). We must walk in intimacy with Jesus so that we're poised to respond to His subtle leadings.

Let me highlight words of knowledge for a moment. Pay attention to various ways that the Holy Spirit may give you a word of knowledge. My prayer partner, Jim Dixon, came to me about nine years ago during a Sunday morning service and said that he was experiencing a particular pain in his body, but he told me that he believed this pain was for someone else. This was the first time that I had encountered a word of knowledge, so I was a bit apprehensive. Yet, I trusted him, so I gave him the microphone. He described his pain and then asked if someone in the service was experiencing that particular pain or injury. Sure enough, someone raised their hand and came forward. After praying for a few moments, this person was completely healed, and at that moment, Jim's pain completely subsided.

Sometimes words of knowledge will be sensed physically, as in the case you just read, but other times you might hear the Spirit whisper something in your heart about someone or something. For example, you might be talking with someone and hear the word "migraine" in your heart. If the person you are talking with has migraines, the Holy Spirit might want you to be the instrument to release His healing to touch that person. Other times you might have a dream about someone or see a picture in your mind. Remember that words of knowledge are *not* for you but for others, so they may not make sense to you initially. If you will trust the Holy Spirit and be willing to step out in faith to release a word of knowledge, you may be surprised how God can use you. Remember, faith is often spelled r-i-s-k.

The question that I am often asked is, "Why would God tell me about someone else's issue? Why doesn't He just heal them directly?" Words of knowledge release faith into people because it assures them that God loves them. A word of knowledge is one of the most tangible ways to demonstrate God's love and concern for people. I know that God loves me, but when someone comes to me and tells me about something that only God and I know, it assures me that He really cares for me. Moreover, it builds and unites the body of Christ. God strengthens His body, the body of Christ, by using people to touch people. In other words, He heals the body *through* the body.

Spiritual gifts, including words of knowledge, manifest for the sake of the body of Christ. The entire assembly is benefited, edified, and strengthened when the Holy Spirit manifests supernatural gifts. I'm reminded about Dan's conversation when someone was being touched by the power of the Spirit, and then they became the instrument that touched someone else. He talked about the entire church ministering "one to another." This should become the normal activity of every church when it flows in the Holy Spirit.

This brings me to the last point I want to highlight, and that is the necessity to be filled with the Holy Spirit and to continue *being* filled with the Spirit (see Ephesians 5:18). I've been reading the accounts of the early Holiness movement in a book entitled *Echoes of the General Holiness Assembly* by S. B. Shaw. This book was written in 1901, and while its pages are worn and falling into pieces, the message is timeless. The book chronicles the accounts of Christians at the turn of the century. The stories I read spoke of the necessity of walking in the Spirit and the possibilities of a Spirit–filled life. Miracles, healings, and accounts of entire sanctification were reported as normal activities of that day. Those believers would not have accepted a life of powerlessness as we have. Sanctification for those Christians was equivalent to a miraculous lifestyle.

Over the years we have drifted into a form of godliness, but we've broken away from the power of the Spirit (see 2 Timothy 3:5). I believe we need to repent and then cry out for a fresh baptism in the Holy Spirit. One of the preachers in that old, tattered book said, "I have often thought I would like to live to see one church of whose membership it could be truly said, 'They were all filled with the Spirit.'"[3] Let every church become an assembly of whose membership is truly filled with the Spirit.

Chapter Four

THE EXTRAORDINARY POWER
OF THE HOLY SPIRIT

J esus said, "But you will receive power when the Holy Spirit has come upon you" (Acts 1:8a). The Bible says, "And with great power the apostles were giving testimony to the resurrection of the Lord Jesus" (Acts 4:33a). Paul said, "For the kingdom of God does not consist in words but in power" (1 Corinthians 4:20). Power was central to Jesus and the early church. The small band of believers in the upper room who were baptized with the Spirit and power seemed impervious to the wiles of the enemy. Historians tells us that within seventy years more than one million people came to Christ—even against the tyranny of Rome. I'm not sure that we could ever know the exact number of people who came to Christ during the first century, but we *do* know that the early Christians prevailed over assaults and persecutions.

There's an interesting book written by a Yale University professor named Ramsay MacMullen and entitled, *Christianizing the Roman Empire A.D. 100–400*. He explores the question,

"How did the early Christians manage to influence so many within a Roman world?" He approaches this question not from an ecclesiastical point of view but purely from a secular and historical view. Therefore, he doesn't write with a purpose to prove the validity of Christianity. He merely explores the historical evidence of what made Christianity so persuasive. His conclusion is rather simple: the early believers operated with supernatural power that was greater than all the gods in Rome.

I hope that we don't excuse ourselves from functioning in divine power by accepting the delusion that extraordinary power is no longer necessary. If what we read about in the book of Acts was the start of the Church—the fledgling, immature beginnings of a movement, then certainly the Church today should be the mature adult in power and authority. Certainly, we should be exceeding what the young "start-up" Church was doing! I hope that Paul's indictment to the Galatians isn't true of believers today, "Having begun by the Spirit, are you now being perfected by the flesh?" (Galatians 3:3).

Power for miracles, deliverance, healing, and salvation is imperative. There is nothing in the Bible that would indicate that believers today should minister absent of the supernatural power of God. My prayer is that, as you read this chapter, you will allow God to stir your heart and fan your passion for more of His Holy Spirit. While this chapter echoes the topic of the last chapter, we will conclude with some pertinent ways to steward a lifestyle of divine power.

Rob: This chapter builds on what we just talked about. I want to discuss the extraordinary power of the Holy Spirit. Let's talk about the supernatural lifestyle because there is no way we can avoid acknowledging it in your ministry. Dan, I read that book by C. B. Jernigan, a former district superintendent in the Church of the Nazarene, entitled *The Pioneer Days of the Holiness Movement in the Southwest*. The book records the accounts of Nazarenes experiencing the extraordinary power of the Holy Spirit. The power of God was so strong that people would shake. Others fell to the ground under His power. On one occasion, people fell under the power of the Holy Spirit one mile away from the revival that was being held in a tent.

Nazarene historian Timothy L. Smith wrote how Phineas F. Bresee swallowed a fire ball, and his lips seemed to burn for three days. I never want to make more of the manifestations than we need to. I never want to glorify them or say that a person has to have these extraordinary encounters. I realize that we don't have to do anything but open our hearts up to Jesus, yet I can't avoid talking about some of these things you have seen. They raise a lot of questions, and sometimes they incite fear and suspicion. So let's just dive into them.

I want you to talk about some of the manifestations of the Spirit you've witnessed. And just let me say that manifestations are nothing new. In 2 Chronicles 5:14 it says the power of God was so heavy that, "The priests could not stand to minister because of the cloud, for the glory of the LORD filled the house of God." The glory filled the house, Dan! Jesus manifested the glory to the extent that when He said "I am He" in John 18:6, the Bible says, "They drew back and fell to the ground." Bud Robinson was preaching, and someone fell out on the saw dust and lay there for two days. John Wesley's ministry was peppered with supernatural encounters, and while Wesley was uncomfortable with them, he never backed down—even when people called him an enthusiast. So what about these manifestations of the Spirit? I know you don't chase after them, but they seem to chase after you. What have you experienced in terms of God's power?

Dan: Honestly, there are too many to talk about in the last three and a half years. I've recorded in my journal over 6,000 people who have fallen under the power of the Spirit, and 10 percent have been ordained elders. Here is a specific occasion that occurred in Sandusky, Ohio. I laid hands on somebody who had been suffering from traumatic nightmares since she was a little girl. She suffered from abuse. I spoke into her as the Spirit prompted me, and she fell on the ground under the power of God. Forty-five minutes later, she got up, and she hasn't had a nightmare since that moment. God supernaturally took her to a place where she was healed and restored.

I prayed for another woman, a retired pastor's wife, in New Mexico. God's power came upon her and she fell out in the Spirit. When she stood up, she was completely restored. Her hope had been renewed. She went back to her seat and got her husband to come up for prayer. God's power healed him from a debilitating condition on his side that remained from a stroke, and he relinquished his walker. I remember when God gave me a word of knowledge for a little nine-year-old girl. She had been abused for four years when she was younger, and she was having nightmares every night. I'll never forget this encounter because the Lord said that He was going to erase her memory of the abuse. I thought that sounded strange, but I said what the Lord told me to her. And this little nine-year-old girl rested under the presence of God. She rested on the floor for forty minutes, and when she stood up, she had no memory of her abuse.

On another occasion I prayed for a thirteen-year-old girl in Ohio. She fell out under the power of the Holy Spirit's presence and lay on the floor for nearly an hour. Later, her parents told me that she was called to be a missionary while under the presence of the Holy Spirit. Recently, I was in Hilliard, Ohio, and I laid hands on a young woman who was really longing for a breakthrough in her life. When the Spirit of God came on her, she couldn't even walk back to her seat. She and her husband called me two days later and told me that the hair on her arms and legs stood up from the moment God came upon her. It was like electric current was going through her.

Four days after this manifestation of the Holy Spirit, she went to the doctors for a scheduled D&C because her fetus had died. However, the baby was alive, and they cancelled the procedure. The doctors had no explanation how the fetus came back to life. I believe the explanation is the direct result of an encounter with the Holy Spirit, and the manifestation of tingling and hair being raised was God touching her.

I can't understand all of this, and I don't chase after it. I just know that nothing is impossible with God. I remember when I was praying for people in Idaho, and many people were falling under the power of the Spirit. It was during this meeting that another lady, who had fallen out in the Spirit, testified that her dead fetus came back to life. I can't explain why this happens, Rob. I don't think you have to fall, you don't have to have goose bumps, and you don't have to have any outward experience to receive a healing. But it does seem that many times there is an outward experience that precedes an inner healing. The ways of God are so mysterious.

To be honest, I used to be afraid and intimidated of the backlash about these things happening. I would try to not saying anything about them because there was controversy about what God was doing. A lot of people have said things about me that stretch things out of proportion and have made things up that aren't true, but in recent months the Lord has asked me, "Why should you be ashamed of what I am doing?" I can't be ashamed anymore, Rob. I have to just walk in step with the Holy Spirit, and if God wants to touch somebody in a supernatural way, then so be it.

I remember when the power of God was flowing in Flint Central Church of the Nazarene, and this little five-year-old boy, who was born deaf, came up to Dr. Gardner and tugged on his coat tail and said, "Pastor, it is too loud. It's too loud." He could hear! God opened up his ears in an atmosphere where people were being touched by the supernatural power of God. I was in Midland, Michigan, and this little nine-year-old boy came up who had cerebral palsy. His name was A.J., and God healed him.

Think about that: the supernatural power of God came on this little guy, and God healed him of cerebral palsy. I believe that there is an unlimited power of God, and the more we are willing to walk in the awareness of the kingdom of God that is in us, the more we can release that reality into the world around us.

When the supernatural power of God falls, some people cry, some people wave their arms, some people laugh, and some people fall down, but it is not about any of these manifestations. In 1 Corinthians 12:6 the Bible talks about the various "effects" of the Spirit of God. There will always be a supernatural effect of the Spirit's outpouring. So we shouldn't worry about *how* people are touched. We just need more people to be touched. I could talk on and on about the various manifestations, Rob. I just know that they are real. It's kind of funny that I've seen all these people get touched across the country, and then just last week at your church there was a man who started jumping up and down. We didn't know what had happened to him, and we didn't know what was wrong with him. All of a sudden, he said, "All my pain is gone in my knees. Both my knees are healed."

Rob: Yes, that's true!

Dan: Then I called that young lady up who just had the second of many surgeries on her birth-defected feet. God instantly touched her, and she started walking with no pain even though the doctor said she couldn't walk for six weeks. She started shouting! These manifestations are real, Rob. I just know that I don't ever want to get in the way of what God is doing. I certainly don't want hype, but I want the kingdom of God to come and His will to be done.

Last night I finished a two-night meeting in northwest Ohio, and there were six churches there including a Wesleyan church and five Nazarene churches. Three of the host pastors went down in the Spirit, and they said that they had never experienced that before but that they knew it was from God. Each of them said that they had never felt closer to God than in that moment when God was resting on them. This happens in every church, and I don't think that we can try to control the Holy Spirit. My desire is that He controls me.

We shouldn't call ourselves a holiness denomination unless we are willing to follow the Holy Spirit's leading. He doesn't have to demonstrate these manifestations, but — for whatever reason — He desires that they happen from time to time. My experience is that when people experience extraordinary manifestations, their fruit remains. There is transformation in their emotions, in their relationships, in their bodies, in their minds, and in their hearts. The fruit remains! So, I'm thankful for the power of God. I don't claim to understand it, but I just don't want to get in His way.

Rob: It is just that, "power!" The Greek word is *dunamis,* and it refers to an extraordinary ability or a supernatural energy. We are afraid of the word energy (Greek *energio*), which is similar to the word for God's power. Unfortunately this word has been stolen by the New Age movement, but the fact remains that there is an energy imparted from God — His power, the power of the Holy Spirit. There is no reason we should spurn this energy and power. I agree that we don't need to chase after these things, but we shouldn't downplay His power either.

Concerning manifestations, I once heard you say, "If we fake them, it is flesh. If we fight them, it is flesh." We just need to let the Holy Spirit do what He wants to do and flow in extraordinary ways however He desires. You know, Dan, I grew up in the late 60s going to the Morse Road Nazarene Campground in Columbus, Ohio. I remember people running, shouting, laughing, crying, and jumping in the Spirit. We didn't think anything of it then. I see manifestations in our history. I see them in the history of the Holiness movement in the late 1800s. There really is nothing new about the outpouring of God's Spirit and His power.

The last thing I want to address is how do you steward the power of God? Obviously, we don't want to highlight *just* His power, but we have to talk about power because people have misunderstood it and people have denied it (see 2 Timothy 3:5). That is why we needed to do a chapter on God's extraordinary power. The question is how do we steward the power of the Holy Spirit?

Dan: I think the only way that one can steward the power of the Holy Spirit is to stay in the place where the Holy Spirit is—that is in the heart of Jesus. The Spirit is poured out through Jesus. Jesus is the Word; therefore, the easiest way I have found is to try to live as much of my life as I can in the Word of God. When we start growing weak in our spirit man, I believe it is because we have stopped feeding our spirit. His Word is Spirit and truth (see John 6:63, 17:17).

I think if we live on a well–prepared, untainted, uncontaminated, and well–balanced diet of God's Word on a daily basis, then we can live on His daily bread, and the result of that will be spiritual energy, spiritual confidence, and spiritual boldness. The anointing of God is tied to time spent with the Word. If we live in the Word, then we are going to pray more because the Word will challenge us. We will find ourselves saying, "Wait a minute. I'm not functioning like I see in the Bible. I need more of His Spirit." Living in the Word will cause us to get closer to God, it will cause us to yearn more for the presence of God, and it is not going to let us be satisfied with "just getting out of here" someday to go to heaven.

We aren't going to be satisfied until we pray and actually see heaven come to earth. We won't rest until we see the kingdom of God manifested here on earth as it is in heaven, and this all starts in the Word. I know that nothing happens without prayer, so I'm not against having prayer meetings. But there has never been a prayer meeting birthed outside of actually believing the Word and doing what it says. When we don't actually believe the Word, it creates this impotence to prayer and crying out. So my main directive from God is that if I want to walk in the power of the Spirit, I need to walk in the power of His Word. Everything that I believe, the paradigms and opinions that I have, and the different theological parameters that guide my life—I find them all in the Word of God. I love His Word.

Rob: It is interesting that you mentioned the prayer of His kingdom coming to earth. This is really an invasion of "another power." It is the king's dominion—the realm of His kingdom invading and touching the kingdom of this earth. His kingdom is superior to ours, so things happen when His kingdom begins to come and flood the earth.

I am thrilled about our conversation concerning the power of God and have witnessed God's power touching people physically, emotionally, and spiritually. While traveling with

Dan, I have personally witnessed four people get out of their wheelchairs. There is no way a person can forget these occurrences. It "ruins" you in the right way because you know what is possible thereafter. I have also seen hundreds, even thousands, of people come to faith or have their hearts purified by the same power of God. I don't ever want to live and minister without the power of God.

Let me underscore four things concerning our conversation about the supernatural power of God. First, Dan mentioned that he received some backlash concerning the demonstration of power. That is to be expected. If you are going to function in the supernatural power of the Holy Spirit, there will always be pushback from people. We've already discussed this in chapter two, but let me reiterate that if you press into the presence of God and the Holy Spirit starts to flow through you in extraordinary ways, you will be criticized.

Years ago, I heard Leonard Ravenhill say, "Most believers live so subnormal that if someone gets baptized in the Spirit and starts to function normal, everyone else will think that they are abnormal." Don't shrink back (Hebrews 10:38). Don't dial it down because of criticism. When boldness got the early church into trouble in the book of Acts, their prayer was for *more* of the kinds of things that got them into trouble to begin with (see Acts 4:29–31). Don't become intimidated and draw back because of backlash from those who don't view God's power as a necessary result of the Spirit's baptism.

Second, we have a tremendous responsibility to steward what has been given to us. Paul stated in 1 Corinthians 4:1 that we are to be regarded as stewards of the mysteries of God. The responsibility of a steward is to manage what has been given to them. We've been given the Holy Spirit, and what accompanies the baptism with the Holy Spirit is power. It is the responsibility of the Church to steward the graces and gifts of God, and we can't point our finger at anyone but ourselves if we're found powerless.

I agree with Cymbala who once stated, "We can't blame the environment for our powerlessness rather than facing our spiritual condition. We talk endlessly about how godless the country is becoming when the only answer to the situation is for us, the church, to return to our spiritual birthright as a powerful community in Jesus Christ."[4] Let's remain in the Spirit. Let's not only walk in the Spirit as Paul commands us in Galatians 5:25, but let's continue to be filled with the Spirit as it says in Ephesians 5:18. Let me add, there is no greater way to remain in the Spirit than to immerse yourself in the Word of God. I couldn't agree more with Dan on that note. If you will get into the Word, it will get into you. So consume the Word every single day.

Third, regarding manifestations of the Spirit, I'm not arguing for or against any particular phenomenon; however, I am stating that when the power of God through the Holy Spirit touches a person, something always happens. Paul said, "But if the Spirit of Him who raised Jesus from the dead dwells in you, He who raised Christ Jesus from the dead will also give life to your mortal bodies through His Spirit who dwells in you" (Romans 8:11). Something is going to happen to our mortal body. Paul said the Spirit is going to give life (*zoopoieo*) to us, a word that means to invigorate, vitalize, or arouse energy inside us.

One expositor said that "life" will always spring forth from inside us when we are touched with the Holy Spirit. The point that I'm making is when the Holy Spirit comes upon a human being, there will probably be a physical response of some kind. There is no possible way to be filled with the Spirit of God and that experience has no effect upon you. Therefore, when you are filled with the power of the Spirit, you might cry, laugh, feel warmth, tingle, dance, shout, tremble, fall, or simply have a sense of peace rest on you. There is no standard response to the initial presence of the Spirit touching you, but something always occurs.

I want you to consider for a moment the various manifestations of God's power as recorded in the Bible. God's power manifested through oil that never ran dry, fires that didn't burn bodies, water that turned to blood, seas that stood straight up, bread that fell from heaven, water that gushed from a rock, a bush on fire but not consumed, a talking donkey, a prophet who road in the belly of a fish, an axe head that floated on water, a flying chariot, hair that stood on edge, water that turned to wine, blind eyes that opened with spittle, dead bodies that emerged from tombs, a lame man who walked after forty years, soldiers being knocked to the ground, a veil torn in two, a virgin getting pregnant, a demon-possessed man delivered and preaching the same day, and a violent storm being calmed.

There are many more examples in the Bible that we could list, but the fact remains, God is an awesome God. When the extraordinary touches the ordinary, something supernatural always occurs. There is a collision between the divine and the human. While there is no set pattern, emotion, or manifestation, when God touches a human being, the Bible, as well as history, is peppered with examples of people falling, shaking, laughing, crying, or a myriad of responses. Best of all, God's power is so extraordinary that it can cleanse our hearts from the propensity of iniquity and enable us to walk in righteousness and holiness.

The last point I want to address regarding manifestations is that they are not new or some strange influence from Pentecostalism. Listen to this journal entry of a particular ministry event:

> The Lord was wonderfully present, more than twenty persons feeling the arrows of conviction. Several fell to the ground; some of whom seemed dead; others, in the agonies of death, the violence of their bodily convulsions exceeding all description. There was also great crying and agonizing in prayer, mixed with deep and deadly groans on every side. . . . It seemed as if the Lord came upon (someone) like a giant, taking him by the neck, and shaking all his bones in pieces. . . . One lay two or three hours in the open air, and being then carried into the house, continued insensible another hour, as if actually dead. The first sign of life she showed was a rapture of praise intermixed with a small joyous laughter.[5]

Someone reading this might label it as an out of control charismatic service when, in reality, it is a journal entry from John Wesley dated July 14, 1759. Although Wesley attempted to downplay these supernatural occurrences, many of his meetings included people weeping, shaking, crying out, losing consciousness, and falling out in the Spirit.[6] On one occasion Wesley asked for God to confirm His power with signs, and, sure enough, during his message the power of God fell on the meeting causing people to manifest and fall to the ground.[7]

Like Dan, all of this is a mystery to me. As to falling out in the Spirit, my only explanation is that God's glory (*kabod*) can be translated as weight. Perhaps the weight of God's presence resting on someone causes them to fall to the ground. I like the explanation of a child who said, "Just as a doctor has to put you to sleep for surgery, so God puts people asleep so He can perform surgery on us." In the final analysis, I just want more of His presence in my life. Therefore, I will receive Him however He chooses to come — even if that means I weep, cry, or laugh or there is no observable manifestation.

Fourth, I want to comment about the focus of the believer. Dan said that when we invest ourselves in the Word, our desires will shift from merely going to heaven to praying and believing that heaven will come to earth. This doesn't mean that a believer won't go to heaven, but we have a mission to complete before considering heaven. Jesus didn't commission us to merely sit around and ponder the spenders of the celestial city, but He commissioned us to make a transformational difference in our world. He sent us into the world to make disciples, to heal the sick, to cast out demons, to cleanse the lepers, and to preach the kingdom.

When the disciples asked Jesus to teach them to pray, Jesus instructed them to pray "thy kingdom come" (Luke 11:2). He didn't tell them to pray about *going* to the kingdom of God but rather to bring His kingdom to earth. We have the privilege and responsibility to usher the King's dominion into our realm. When that happens, demonic strongholds are cast down and demolished (2 Corinthians 10:4–5). We have the authority in Christ to displace the realm of darkness through the mighty power of God.

In fact, the kingdom of God is in you (Luke 17:21). Therefore, everywhere you go you carry the realm of the supernatural within you. When you walk into a room of a sick person, the odds shift in your favor. You and Jesus are a majority, and you carry within you the dominion of your King. So don't be surprised what might happen when you lay hands on someone and declare sickness to flee. Don't be shocked when you place your hands on someone and ask for an increase of the Spirit of God to rest on them. Wherever you go, you have the privilege to release the presence of God. You disperse the heavenly realm over earthly situations, and when that occurs, there will be a demonstration of God's power. You may not see it in the physical realm, but rest assured that something supernatural is taking place.

Chapter Five

THE MINISTRY OF IMPARTATION

Several years ago, I had lunch with a district superintendent in the Church of the Nazarene. We had a pleasant conversation, but his interest circled the topic of impartation. He attended a conference that Dan and I led and we concluded the conference with an impartation. So he was inquisitive about this particular subject matter. I was glad to answer questions and I also was also encouraged that he desired to learn more about the ministry of impartation.

I believe impartations are vital to the ongoing ministry of the church. Not everyone feels the same, however, about this subject. Not too long ago, a pastor sent my district superintendent a letter stating his concerns over an impartation service I was involved in. He believed that it was a charismatic influence and he stated concerns that I was misleading people to participate in something that wasn't in the Bible. I cannot deny that the Charismatic movement, as well as Pentecostals, practice the ministry of impartation, but I can assure you that they weren't the first ones to practice it. The Bible is filled with examples of impartation.

One of the first impartations in the Bible is in Numbers chapter eleven. God approached Moses and told him that He was going to take the Spirit that was on Moses and transfer (impart) that onto seventy other people. The Bible says that Joshua was filled with the spirit of wisdom because Moses laid hands on him (Deuteronomy 34:9). Apparently, Moses imparted — gave — something to Joshua.

Elijah transferred an anointing onto Elisha (2 Kings 2:9–15) and the apostles transferred something onto Barnabas and Saul before they were sent out (Acts 13:3–4). When Jesus told His disciples to wait in Jerusalem until they were clothed with power, they were waiting for an impartation. God was about to impart His Spirit upon them so that they could be empowered to function in the ministry. When I was ordained in 1992, a general superintendent laid hands on my head and imparted a mantle of authority upon me to minister in the Church of the Nazarene. These are all examples of the ministry of impartation.

Because there is such widespread ignorance about this subject matter, especially among Nazarenes, Dan and I decided to include this subject to our discussion. Moreover, Dan has seen enormous fruit through the ministry of impartation, and it's necessary to shed light on what God is doing. I believe that God is going to give you a spirit of wisdom and revelation about this imperative ministry. In fact, if you will open your heart and humbly receive, I believe that you will receive an impartation by reading this chapter.

Rob: As we begin our discussion about the ministry of impartation, let's define what we mean by the word "impartation." It simply means to impart or to give. Paul talked about his desire to impart or to give a supernatural gift to the Christians in Rome (Romans 1:11). He actually said that his impartation would "establish" them. While the word impartation is a mystery to a lot of people, it is just a word that means to give (*metadidomi*). If I give you something—a pen or water, I am imparting something to you. I realize that there is a lot of controversy about this subject matter, so I'm praying that God will help us.

Dan: There is, Rob. There's a lot of fear and confusion over this subject.

Rob: I want to start with my life because even before I knew about the ministry of impartation, things started happening in and through me when I got around certain people. I told you about my sabbatical and what I experienced. That was an impartation from God. I was already born again and baptized in the Spirit, but God gave me an impartation. He imparted an increase of His presence upon me. I would describe my encounter with God during my sabbatical as a baptism of

His love. God extended grace to me during those weeks that I spent with Him. He laid His hands on me, and I will forever be different.

I believe the first time that I met you, Dan, I received an impartation. The day that I met you, you were saying things from the Word that I didn't even know were in the Bible. I had been through college and seminary, I've had Bible training, and still you were teaching me about God's Word. Listening to you speak made me so hungry. I wanted to be a man of the Word. I wanted to know the Bible like you did. And after you left, I laid on the floor for two hours, saying to God, "I want to know the Word. I want to know the Scripture like Dan." I was just so hungry to have the Word jammed in me like you did. God has answered that hunger.

A few months after meeting you, I was praying at my church and the Word just started coming to me. I now have an insatiable desire for the Scripture. As a result of that impartation, I've learned that if I get into the Word, the Word gets into me. As I study the Word, it studies me. As I declare the Word, it declares my life. I'm committed to studying the Word every single day. That was an impartation I received from you, and it comes out in my preaching, it comes out in my praying, and it comes out in my conversations. I simply love the Word.

About a year after my sabbatical, as we were searching for language to describe the events at our church, our staff attended a Healing and Impartation School led by Randy Clark. I had never heard of him before, but he talked about impartations and about receiving a greater anointing. He encouraged us to realize that we can always have more of the Holy Spirit. John 3:34 says, "He gives the Spirit without measure," and Luke 11:13b says, "How much more will your heavenly Father give the Holy Spirit to those who ask Him?" In Ephesians 5:18, the word "filled" is a present tense verb, which means "drinking," "receiving," and "filling" with the Holy Spirit.

Randy talked about the fact that God wanted to give an impartation to people, but there were two things we should know before he prayed for us. First, receiving was conditioned upon hunger. He said that God would pour out upon us to the measure of our hunger for Him. Second, we needed to be willing to do whatever God wanted us to do when we received an impartation because our lives belonged entirely to God. As he taught the morning session and I sat there with my staff and about four-hundred people, my heart started pounding because I didn't even want to hear the rest of his message. I just wanted an increase of God in my life.

Randy was talking about receiving more of God and I was so hungry that I needed to go forward even before he gave the invitation. I thought what will these people think, what will my staff think, and I didn't want to interrupt his message, but I just wanted God to touch me. Obviously, I didn't need a person named Randy to touch me, but I knew at that moment God was using him, God's minister, as a vessel to pour something upon me that God wanted me to have in my life. So in front of four-hundred people, I went up and interrupted his message with my hands held out ready to receive. We have already talked about the manifestations, but I remember that Randy blew on me like Jesus did His disciples (see John 20:22).

Dan: That's funny.

Rob: Listen, he blew on me, and I fell on the ground and couldn't move for about forty-five minutes! I remember people started coming forward and were standing around me, but I was incapacitated. I was resting in God's presence. I was out, Dan! I couldn't move! I remember thinking that if my staff told anyone what happened to me, I would fire them.

Finally, when I was able to stand up, Randy laid hands on me and started praying a prophetic prayer that I would be used by God to redig the wells in the Holiness movement. I didn't know what that meant. I really had no clue at the time, but something in my heart came alive. My heart started to feel like it was on fire. About twenty minutes later, he found my wife, and he prophesied the same thing over her. That was an impartation that has forever changed my life. That is what I'm doing with the rest of my life, Dan. I'm redigging the wells.

Dan: Amen, Rob!

Rob: That was in January of 2008, and within a year of that impartation and prophetic prayer I began traveling. As you know, God has opened up many doors of ministry outside my local church. I have seen God do some amazing things in my meetings, and I almost always include impartations. Since that time, I've written a book and three workbooks and God is helping me to develop resources for pastors and leaders. Some of my resources have already gone into different countries, Dan. The wells are being redug!

Dan: Praise God! That's so amazing.

Rob: I want to be quick to state that I'm not doing what Randy told me to do, but I am doing what God said. Randy just happened to be the key God used to unlock the plans of God that He placed in my heart. That was an impartation, that was an encounter, and that was an unforgettable moment in the presence of God. So, all of these things I've mentioned are impartations: God touching me in Summersville, West Virginia, the power of God I received from you when we met the first time that gave me an insatiable desire for the Word, and then the encounter that I had with Randy.

These are moments that are very significant in my life and yet, there remains a mystery to them. There is something unexplainable about the laying on of hands and about impartations! There is something significant to Paul's words in 1 Timothy 4:14 about "laying on of hands" or in 2 Timothy 1:6, "kindle afresh the gift of God which is in you through the laying on of my hands." My life has been radically touched by God using people like you, Randy, and others who have put their arms around me or have laid their hands on me and prayed for me. You have had an imparta-tion and you now give yourself to the ministry of impartation. Talk to me about that. Tell me how it started with you and your experiences with this ministry.

Dan: Well, the first obvious impartation was when Jesus came to my hospital bed and totally transformed my life. He touched me and gave me an impartation Himself. Since then I have had many times in the desert of isolation seeking God, and He has come to me many times. But about two years ago, I was with my friend Corey Jones in Fort Worth, Texas. He is a great apostle of prayer, and he calls people to corporate prayer.

I had a dream while at Corey's house. It was a Thursday night. In my dream revival broke out at his church, and it continued on for several weeks. God TV called Corey, and they put the revival meeting on television. In my dream the revival was going around the world seven nights a week. People were coming from all over the world, and they were being saved, sanctified, and healed. They were receiving impartations and going back to their churches with the power of the Spirit and imparting that power into their countries, and revivals were breaking out around the world.

When I woke up from the dream, I thought this was the strangest dream I have ever had — this little church experiencing a revival and people coming from all over the world. Friday morning, the morning after the dream, I was sharing the dream with Corey and Beth Ann. Their vision is to see revival, too. They want to see the world touched by the power of God. So as I'm sharing my dream with them, at about 10:30 a.m., the same gentleman who prayed an impartation over you, Rob, called me and wanted to pray an impartation over me. Randy Clark called me, and he said that he had heard about me and what God was doing in the Nazarene tribe. He learned how people were being sanctified, healed, and delivered.

He prayed for a thousandfold increase in my ministry, and he prayed that the demonic realm would be pushed back, the kingdom of God would come, and revival would break out wherever I went. He prayed that the healings and miracles Jesus did with His disciples would start occurring in the Church of the Nazarene and beyond.

Rob: Dan, the exact night you had that dream at Corey's house about revival I had an interesting dream, too. I was in Dayton, Ohio. At the time, I was part of a cohort of eighteen people pursuing my doctorate and Randy Clark was one of my group members. As you were dreaming about revival, I had a dream that I was going to be standing beside Randy and you were going to call me, and when you did, I handed the phone to Randy and he prayed over you. The next morning you called me, and I happened to be standing next to Randy! When your picture popped up on my phone, I remembered the dream that I had. So I said to Randy, "Hey, why don't you call my friend and bless him." So I gave him my phone and that's when he called you.

Dan: Wow! That's so amazing! That's hard for people to believe.

Rob: It is. What are the chances of that? That's life in the Spirit of God, Dan. Only God can do these kinds of things. He orchestrates things to advance His kingdom, and if we'll remain in the Spirit, we get to become the instruments He uses.

Dan: I will never forget the feeling when he called me. It was like, wow! You know, I never have had any of my colleagues or Nazarenes in my tribe want to pray an impartation on me. It made me start to think: Why would someone who is not even affiliated with my denomination want to pray an impartation upon me? Why would someone who doesn't even know me feel led to pray an impartation on me the morning after I just had a dream for worldwide revival?

Rob: That's a good question. I think many in our denomination avoid impartations because of fear and lack of understanding; therefore, they aren't in a place to be used by God in that manner. I believe that if we're hungry for more of God, He will put people in our path to bring spiritual increase. Because of your hunger for God, He led Randy to you. I also believe that this is an example of how the walls are coming down between denominations. But it has to change though. We need to start embracing the ministry of impartation.

Dan: We really do!

Rob: So what kinds of things started happening after your impartation?

Dan: The next few weeks after Randy's prayer were amazing. I immediately went to this revival in Waco, Texas. I had a word of knowledge for someone's stomach and the lady was completely healed. In that same meeting, someone's deaf ear was opened. Then I went to Wichita Falls, Texas, and during that meeting a little boy's eyes were healed and he was able to see.

From there, I went to Tyler, Texas, and prayed over a man with Parkinson's disease, and he was touched. He was completely healed and stopped shaking. Then I went to Ovilla, Texas, where I saw a lady get out of a wheelchair. In Athens, Texas, God's power fused the heel bone of the worship leader. After that meeting, I went to Gilmore, Texas, and the pastor's back was healed. In Denison, Texas, a lady's arms were healed from nerve damage. While in Odessa, Texas, a seventy-year-old woman with neuropathy was healed. In Belton, Texas, a retired district super-intendent's cancer was healed.

I started seeing all these miracles occurring more rapidly, and I didn't even think anything about it until I looked back on my impartation. I believe that the prayer Randy prayed over me had an effect on me because I was so hungry for more of God's power in my life to touch people for Jesus' sake. I was so hungry to touch people for the sake of the gospel that the seed of his prayer took root deep in my heart. I think when an impartation comes, the only way it takes root in you is that you have to be so hungry for more of God and hungry for Him to manifest His dream through you. If you're not hungry, an impartation won't take root.

Rob: Absolutely, I couldn't agree more. This is why there are people who walk away unchanged from services saturated with the presence of God. They don't come with hungry hearts. I also believe this is why some people spurn impartations. They really aren't hungry and desperate for more of His presence in their lives, so they reject the idea that God wants to give them an increased anointing.

Dan: It's true, blessings come to those who hunger and thirst. God is attracted to our hunger for Him.

Rob: He is, Dan. That's so true. And the Bible is full of examples of that, such as the Syrophoenician woman who wouldn't leave Jesus alone (see Matthew 15:21–28).

Dan: I like Luke 6:19a where it says, "And all the people were trying to touch Him." These people were desperate. They were hungry, so they were seeking after Him. Nothing else mattered to these people but getting to Jesus so that He could *touch* them, which literally means to "set on fire." Jesus went on to say that the kingdom is given to those who are poor in spirit (Luke 6:20). In other words, those who are desperate and hungry gain the kingdom.

Rob: Yes, that's good.

Dan: I started to realize that something was different because of my impartation. Last year when I was praying at Christmas time, before I started my 2015 year, God specifically spoke to me. By the way, when I get to November of this year (2015), it will be seven years of full-time traveling ministry. Anyway, every Christmas break I pray and ask God for His direction for the coming year. God gave me two specific mandates for this year of 2015.

First, He wanted me to live in the Gospels and the book of Acts. He told me to read about Jesus' life and the disciples' life of ministry so that I would become more acclimated to the New Testament DNA. So every week, since the beginning of this year, I've read the gospels and the book of Acts. Second, God told me to do impartations everywhere I go. I initially thought, "Okay, God. And how in the world is that going to happen because I have never even heard of that in Nazarene circles?" But the more I started studying this topic and thinking about it, the more I realized that it had to be taught and implemented.

Rob: What kinds of things has God taught you?

Dan: It's interesting to note that the writer of Hebrews called "laying on of hands" an elementary function (see Hebrews 6:2). So obviously, the first century church knew something about "laying on of hands." It wasn't something that was mysterious or weird, but it was something that was ordinary and accepted.

In the book of Acts there are many different encounters people experienced. People would receive the Word when the apostles would teach, which is like an impartation. In Acts chapter eight, Philip went into the city of Samaria and he was imparting the Word. As a result, demons were cast out of people and various diseases were healed. Paralyzed and lame people were touched by the power of God, and they received Jesus. But there were greater impartations still to come. Peter and John, after learning about Philip's ministry experiences, came to Samaria because they wanted to lay hands on all the new believers. This impartation wasn't to ordain them for ministry like we think — as in a formal sense, but they wanted to lay hands on these new Christians so that they would receive the Holy Spirit. This was an impartation of a greater anointing (see Acts 8:17).

The same thing happened in Acts 19 when Paul found some disciples in Ephesus. The first question out of his mouth was, "Did you receive the Holy Spirit when you believed?" (Acts 19:2). They responded by saying that they didn't even know that there was a Holy Spirit, so Paul led them into repentance and baptism in the name of Jesus and then he laid hands on them so that they could receive the Holy Spirit. Paul gave them an impartation. The more that I studied the Word, the more I realized that you don't have to have someone's hands on you to receive an impartation, but it most certainly is one way to receive from God.

If you think about it, Randy prayed for me, but he didn't lay hands on me. Rob, what you said about your impartation of the Word when you met me is something I've had people tell me in almost every church I go to. When I leave a church, people have an increased desire to be in the Word, but I don't lay hands on them for that. What I'm saying is that impartations can happen through prayer, through a sermon, through a song, or through laying on of hands. We just need to be hungry and willing to receive whatever God wants to give us and receive it however He wants to impart to us.

Here's something else I've learned about impartations: God will give what we are full of. The *real* question is what are we full of? In John 20, Jesus said that He was going to send His disciples out just as the Father had sent Him. After He said that, He breathed on His disciples. I believe that is a template for impartation. I don't think that we are required to go around and literally breathe on people, but I believe that we are supposed to release what we are full of. Jesus released the Holy Spirit because He was filled with the Spirit, and if we are really full of the Holy Spirit, then our passion will be to give Him away to others. Our lives will release the presence of God on others because His Spirit will flow out of us.

Rob: That's excellent. So tell me about this year of doing impartations.

Dan: Obedient to God's Word, I began this year praying for impartations, and the first church that I was in was Web City, Missouri. There was an eighty-seven-year-old retired pastor who couldn't walk without a walker. I laid hands on him during an impartation, and God fell on him. He started running around the sanctuary. He was completely healed. When I was in Wichita Falls, Texas, there was a visiting pastor in the service that received an impartation. He had a concussion from a car wreck and had lost all sense of taste for over two years. After the impartation, God restored his ability to taste food again. The next day, he went to the hospital to pray for one of his parishioners, and he said that he felt a tingling of God's presence flowing though his arms as he prayed. That power of God was released into the person at the hospital as this pastor prayed for them.

I've done impartations in every church this year so far, and I can't believe what I am hearing from the people. Churches are being touched by the power of God. People are living in a culture of revival. I'm hearing later that the people in these churches have more faith, have more boldness, and see signs of the kingdom breaking out in different ways inside and outside of the church. In my personal life, I believe the ministry of impartation is a New Testament ministry.

My father–in–law, Dr. Don Owens, says there is something to this ministry of "laying on of hands." He believes that sometimes we limit God's work to when we only lay hands on someone who is sick or someone who is being ordained for ministry. He believes that there is something profound about people, who are full of the Spirit, laying hands on others to receive *more* of that Spirit.

Rob: Well, something gets transferred when we do.

Dan: Yes, I believe that. An impartation releases the manifestation of the Spirit, and by releasing the Spirit, there are multiple things that can occur. I believe people can be called to ministry, they can receive different supernatural gifts, they can receive an increased awareness of the Spirit in their lives, and they can be healed. I have had people testify that they have been sanctified during an impartation. There is an unlimited number of things the Holy Spirit can do if we are just willing to believe.

Rob: How do you do impartations? What do you say? How do they work?

Dan: I usually do them at the end of the service after I've done some teaching on it. But before I call people forward to pray an impartation over them, I give them two warnings. Obviously, people have to be hungry to receive from God. I don't force anyone to receive an impartation. People have to desire more of God, or, otherwise, an impartation is fruitless.

The first warning I give to people before an impartation is they must be willing to do whatever God
says. If we remain in our old wine skins, the new
wine will ruin us (see Luke 5:37). Jesus actually
says that we can't put new wine in old wine skins.
So people must be willing to adjust their lives
according to God's ways. They must be willing
to throw their old paradigms away and let God
design new ones. If people aren't willing to do
that, they will not be blessed with an increase of
the Holy Spirit, but they will become frustrated
and disillusioned. God gives the Holy Spirit to
everybody who obeys Him (see Acts 5:32). So I
tell people that they must be radically obedient
to do whatever God says.

The second warning I give to people is they must
be willing to go wherever God desires to send
them. When I was standing at the gas pump in
Laramie, Wyoming, and God spoke to me about
traveling and preaching, that was in impartation
of God's Spirit resting on me. But I didn't know
that I was going to live the next six years and
seven months away from my wife, four children,
and twelve grandchildren. My cross is my life of
loneliness. I didn't realize that when God put His
anointing on me to do this ministry, He was going
to ask me live away from those I love most. So I
warn people, if you really want the impartation of

God's Spirit on your life, don't ask for all of God if you aren't willing to give Him all of you.

Rob: That is excellent advice, Dan.

Dan: That is what I tell people every time. I have done impartations everywhere, and it has been received everywhere with no controversy when it is presented in the Spirit and backed up with the Word. The controversy only occurs when people don't know the Word. There are many people who call themselves students of the Word, but they don't even know what is actually in the Word. I don't judge people, but I want people to have a greater encounter with Jesus. I believe the world is dying for His manifest presence to bring transformation to their lives, their families, their marriages, their bodies, their churches, and their cities. So I believe impartations should be one of the main things that Spirit–filled Christians should be involved in.

You don't have to call it "impartation." Whether you call it loving your brother, making disciples, giving away Jesus, or whatever you want, I just use the word impartation because it is in Romans 1:11. It's what Paul wanted to do with the believers in Rome. Ever since I have been filled with the Holy Spirit, I have wanted to give

Jesus away. When the disciples in Acts 6 were overwhelmed with all the necessities of feeding people and helping people with their tangible needs, they appointed seven men known to be full of the Holy Spirit to wait on those personal needs so that they could devote themselves to prayer and the ministry of the Word. The Word is Jesus. If we invest our lives in prayer and the ministry of the Word, we're going to be full of Jesus. If we're full of Jesus, our desire will be to serve Him up to everyone we meet. Our lives will become an "all you can eat" buffet of Jesus.

I just want more of the presence of God in my life so that I'm willing to give away all He has given to me. Then others can give away what they've received, and the ministry of impartation can continue on. That is a life of impartation. I believe in it and I think it is necessary. It is an essential way that God has chosen to pour Himself out upon His people.

Rob: You know, Dan, you already mentioned this, but Jesus says in Matthew 12:34 that your mouth will speak what your heart is full of. I think we are always giving away something. It might be negativity, anger, frustration, or gossip, or we are giving away Jesus. I think it is interesting because our lives are *always* giving away impartations that are either good or bad. We are always releasing *something* from our lives. It's like a cup that's being shaken. What spills out of the cup is not determined by the shaking, but rather what spills out of the cup is determined by the contents that are inside. If we are filled with Holy Spirit, then when we are shaken, that is what will spill out—no doubt.

Whenever I am around Corey Jones, I want to pray with a greater passion because that is what spills from his life. He is giving away an impartation of prayer and intercession because he is filled with that passion. In fact, I believe if we are hungry and can honor the anointing that is on certain people, God will release what they carry onto us. That is why I believe God gave me a hunger for the Word when I met you. I realized that you carried a passion and fervor for the Word and that transferred to me. I pray more effectively because of being around Corey. It transferred to me. I have a desire to prophesy like my friend Kevin Seymour and present the gospel like Dr. Charles "Chic" Shaver because I've been around these guys. What they carry has transferred to me because I'm hungry for more of God, and I honor what they carry. I desire to be used by God in greater ways.

Dan: And it doesn't have anything to do with being jealous but rather staying humble and hungry.

Rob: There is one last thing I want to say in regard to an impartation. This might be more of a caution, but sometimes people are asking for a forest and God gives them an acorn. We shouldn't ever be disappointed by what God gives us in an impartation. What I mean by that is sometimes an impartation comes to us like small seeds — almost like God is saying, "You can have the forest, but I'm going to start you out with one acorn." Does that make sense?

Dan: Absolutely.

Rob: When we are praying an impartation over people, I believe that God always gives them something. He always places something on them when they come forward and we lay hands on them, but sometimes instead of the forest God gives them an acorn. The challenge they have is to steward what they've been given into an increase. If a person will nurture and steward what God gives them, it will multiply. I believe that is the principle behind the parable of the talents (see Matthew 25:14–29; Luke 19:11–26).

In fact, sometimes when I teach on the ministry of impartation, I use the analogy of seeds being planted in soil. If the ground is fertile and the seeds are fertilized, nurtured, and cared for, they are going to grow into a harvest. There will be an increase of what has been sown. So we can't despise small beginnings (see Zechariah 4:10). I want to increase and steward what God has given me through Randy and many others, and I believe you desire the same.

Dan: Yes and amen!

I hope this chapter has been helpful to your understanding of the ministry of impartation. When God spoke through Isaiah about His covenant in Isaiah 59:21, He said that the blessing of the covenant would extend from generation to generation, from offspring to offspring. This is an implication of what an impartation is. We have a responsibility to transfer what God gives us to those around us.

Years ago when I was in high school, I used to run the 440 relay. I received a baton from someone who ran behind me for a quarter of a lap. When I received the baton, it was my turn to run for a quarter of a lap. It would have been ridiculous and foolish to turn around and "rerun" the same path that my fellow teammate ran. Moreover, I would have been disqualified. I was to take the baton beyond the distance of the exchange. Spiritual impartations are moments when God places upon us anointing, revelations, callings, or supernatural gifts, and we are to exceed past generations. We should extend the spiritual territory our spiritual mothers and fathers once walked upon.

Another critical component was handing the baton onto the next person. Our coach trained us in this procedure over and over again so that when game time arrived, we would successfully pass the baton on to the next person. Passing the baton on is similar to the ministry of impartation. We are passing on to others what God has given to us. Jesus said, "Freely you have received, freely give" (Matthew 10:8b). I hope that we will give ourselves to this ministry. For pastors and leaders interested in praying an impartation over others, it's as simple as praying that God will transfer your blessings onto others. We are always blessed to bless others. We are never to hoard what God gives us, but we are to generously give to others. So feel free to call people forward, pray blessings over them, and impart to them what has been given to you. I want to highlight three aspects that will help you before leaving this chapter.

First, I cannot overstate the importance of living with a hunger for more of God. Hunger really is the essence of humility because hunger acknowledges that we have a need. Hunger acknowledges that we haven't arrived yet and we're still pressing into God for more—more love, more power, more of the Spirit, more faith, more power, and more of His presence in our lives. Only humble people will come forward for an impartation. Only hungry people will even admit that they require more. God will place people in the path of hungry people whom He will use to impart the increase you desire.

So, how do you stay hungry? Consume the Word, eat spiritual truths, and lean into the Holy Spirit. In the natural realm, I eat and then I'm full, but in the spiritual realm, I eat and I get hungrier. You will increase your appetite for God when you consume spiritual truths. So immerse yourself in God's Word. Meditate and stuff your mind with the right things (see Philippians 4:8). Keep your mind set on spiritual things, and don't get overwhelmed with worldly things (see Colossians 3:2).

Second, steward whatever God gives you. Increase comes to those who put to use what God places into their hands. If you're a pastor, be the best one you can be. If you're a worship leader, be the best one you can be. If you teach a group lesson, teach the best you can. When you go to your job, be the best worker you can be. Give yourself to the task and assignment that God has given you and work as unto the Lord (see Colossians 3:23). Don't complain that you aren't gifted or used like someone else. Do what God has called you to do, and do it with no complaints. God has divided His "possessions" to all of us (see Matthew 25:14). The question is will we invest what He has given to us, or will we bury it in the ground out of fear and laziness?

Third, be willing to allow those you pray for to increase beyond you. Jesus said that the works He did would be exceeded by those who would follow Him (John 14:12). We must be secure enough in our walk with Jesus to allow others to rise higher in their spiritual calling. Using the 440 relay illustration again, we must be willing to applaud people when they run beyond us. They are supposed to increase beyond our distance.

We will talk about this in the next chapter, but this is what an apostolic environment is all about. It's an environment filled with spiritual fathers and mothers who impart to spiritual children so they can grow and surpass their spiritual parents (see 1 Corinthians 4:15). Don't ever hold people back out of insecurity and jealousy. Celebrate the victories that those around you have. If King Saul would have applauded David's successes instead of becoming jealous, it would have elevated his own life. He would have risen in the applause for the one that he honored; instead, Saul sank in envy and eventually lost his anointing and position.

Dan and I have both been blessed by the ministry of impartation. We've been recipients of God's touches, and we've had the privilege to bless others in services where we've prayed impartations on people. There's a book you should purchase in the selected reading section by Randy Clark entitled *There is More: Reclaiming the Power of Impartation*. It's a great book that will help instruct you in this important ministry. I am believing for more to be given to all those who have read this chapter. May God do "far more abundantly beyond all that we ask or think" (Ephesians 3:20).

Chapter Six

AN APOSTOLIC CULTURE:
A BIBLICAL MODEL FOR MINISTRY

A few years ago, I held a revival in Texas and as the host pastor drove us back to his house, we discussed the apostolic fivefold ministry model in the Bible. Before we go any further, let me explain what I mean by the apostolic fivefold ministry model. The Bible says, "And He gave some as apostles, and some as prophets, and some as evangelists, and some as pastors and teachers" (Ephesians 4:11). There are five distinct callings or offices identified in this verse: apostles, prophets, evangelists, pastors, and teachers. So when I use the word fivefold, I am referring to these five callings. Together, they are called an apostolic team because they all work cooperatively for one reason, and that is to equip God's people to do ministry (Ephesians 4:12).

Equipping is a "sending" assignment. We send or deploy people to do ministry inside and outside of the church walls. The word apostolic refers to a sending role that each of these offices is required to do. The fivefold equips the saints of God so that people can be deployed into ministry. Whenever we send God's people into ministry, we are involved in apostolic work. The Greek word for "sent" is *apostello*, and this means to set apart, to appoint, to send out, or to send off. Missionaries, for example, who have been deployed to another country have been *apostello* or sent. By and large, a missionary has learned under the influence of a pastor or teacher — maybe an evangelist, and they were equipped. Therefore, a missionary has experienced an apostolic influence even if they didn't know it.

Returning to my conversation with this pastor, we were discussing the apostolic fivefold model that is recorded in the book of Ephesians. He agreed that we have embraced the role of an evangelist, pastor, and teacher, but we haven't understood or embraced the idea that God still calls apostles and prophets. Our three hour conversation was very refreshing, but we both realized that a lot of work is still needed to help many of us adequately function in a fivefold leadership model.

The pushback I often hear to the fivefold ministry model is twofold. First, I hear that God no longer calls apostles and prophets because we have the Bible and the Church has been established. My response to this statement is because we have the Bible, we should realize what it says so that we can help the established Church. The Bible doesn't indicate that the role of the apostle or prophet has been suspended. In fact, it argues otherwise. The Bible says, "And God has appointed in the church, first apostles, second prophets, third teachers" (1 Corinthians 12:28a). This appointment is by God, and there is no expiration date on it.

The second rebuff I receive is that a church cannot financially support all five offices. Someone once argued with my wife stating that most churches cannot afford to pay these five positions. Who said anything about paying them? Others have stated that God only calls pastors to lead a church, so only pastors should be paid. I would argue that we have adopted that model (a senior pastor over a church) because we are used to that wine skin.

What I find interesting is that some of these same churches will hire a youth pastor, seniors' pastor, children's pastor, visitation pastor, or a worship pastor. And in some cases, each of these positions draws a salary, too. My point is that we employ leaders based on what we view as necessary, and in reality I can't find any of those offices in the Bible. How can we disparage apostles and prophets when those positions are peppered throughout God's Word? Paul, an apostle, didn't travel with a youth pastor, but he traveled with a prophet named Silas (Acts 15:32 and 40).

Moreover, if a local church is truly the body of Christ, then don't you think God will lead or call the kinds of leaders into that body to thoroughly equip it? God wants the body of Christ to be built up (see Ephesians 4:12). Just as God might call someone to a local church to work with the youth as a youth pastor, so He might call an evangelist within the same church to equip people to reach out or a prophet to equip people to function prophetically in the Spirit. That same church might have a God–called apostle who equips people to think beyond the walls of the church and a teacher who equips people in the Word. How can one single pastor accomplish the task of equipping the saints to do the work of ministry? I believe if we are sensitive to the Holy Spirit, we will find that He will not only give us leaders for our youth, children, and senior adults, but He will call apostles, prophets, evangelists, and teachers to our side as well.

This chapter may be a paradigm shift for some of you. Please read it with your heart turned toward the Holy Spirit. In the end, I hope that you are encouraged to think outside of the ecclesiastical box that's we've been reared in. Our local churches and denominations need to think through this apostolic fivefold model. As long as we utilize earthly leadership models, we will never experience heavenly results. It's time to let the Holy Spirit give us revelation into a new biblical model.

Rob: Dan, in this section I want to talk about building a biblical model for ministry in our churches. I remember a few years ago when I was reading through Ephesians and came to this verse 4:11–12, "And He gave some *as* apostles, and some *as* prophets, and some *as* evangelists, and some *as* pastors and teachers, for the equipping of the saints for the work of service, to the building up of the body of Christ." I looked at that last verse, ". . . the equipping of the saints for the work of ministry to the building up of the body of Christ."

The only way the body of Christ is going to be built is if people do the works of service, and the only way they can do the works of service is if they have been equipped. The question is how are the people of God going to be adequately equipped if we don't have apostles, prophets, evangelists, pastors, and teachers?

You and I both were reared in the church that had a "threefold" ministry setting, we gave credence to evangelists, pastors, and teachers, but we didn't acknowledge apostles and prophets. Talk to me about this. What are you seeing across the land? What are you seeing, and what are your thoughts about apostles, prophets, evangelists, pastors, and teachers?

Dan: What I'm seeing is that most pastors who operate under a nominal or institutional paradigm void of the fivefold are discouraged and looking for the next ray of hope. They are tired of leadership conferences and management seminars. I think there is a problem in the system and structure of our church, Rob. I believe the last research I read in a couple of books was that around 1,600 to 1,700 pastors leave the ministry each month. Listen to this: over half of all pastors in ministry would leave the pastorate if they could find another way of supporting their family because they feel burned out. I think it is a systemic problem affecting churches across the country. We are trying to do things from a government of man instead of a government of God.

There are these old wine skin churches that have operated with this institutional mindset for years, which may have worked in the past, but it's time to get back to a biblical model. Our institutional mindset really has more to do with us than what the Bible actually says. In my studies, I have been exploring missiology and church growth around the planet, and 80 percent of all church growth is happening where apostolic governments are functioning and not denominational governments. In these churches that are operating apostolically, the leaders of these churches have 10,000 plus members in size, and some even have 100,000 people or more.

Also, many of the leaders of these churches have only a 6th, 7th, or 8th grade education, but they have had encounters with the Holy Spirit. They have an anointing on them where they are not going to conferences to learn leadership, management, or man's techniques, but instead they are seeking the Holy Spirit and being led by the Spirit's techniques. Think about that: 80 percent of the churches that are growing around the globe have no denominational governmental paradigm, but they function with the apostolic kingdom government paradigm. We need to pay attention to what the Bible says about structure or leadership models.

Rob: So how does the fivefold work? I know that they are supposed to equip the saints, but what are the functions of each one?

Dan: I believe apostles *govern*. They hear what is going on in the heavenly realm because God has given them a special calling to see from the perspective of heaven. They have the responsibility of oversight. They give messages that give guidance and oversight for movements. They have the anointing to bring corporate shifts because they operate from the perspective of the heavenly realm, and so they have great vision and insight as to where churches and movements need to go. We might think of apostles as spiritual fathers, too. They father/parent movements.

I believe prophets *guide*. They have the ability to see and hear prophetically, so they give words of guidance. Prophets have the ability to alert churches and movements of where the Spirit is leading. They can avert spiritual disaster, too. Sometimes their words bring correction or

warning to movements. If the Church is operating with evangelists, pastors, and teachers but
not prophets and apostles, then we are operating
in a realm that keeps chasing itself around in the
earthly realm without the heavenly influence.
This is why I believe God appointed them in the
Church first (see 1 Corinthians 12:28). They keep
the church attached to the spiritual realm. They
help funnel in supernatural activities.

Rob: That's good. That might be why we don't
see much supernatural activity in our churches.

Dan: It is, Rob. The job of the apostles and
prophets is to help us become aware of the atmosphere of the kingdom, and if we don't recognize
them or acknowledge them, then supernatural
activity isn't as prevalent. So, apostles govern
and prophets guide.

Next are evangelists and they *gather*. I don't know
very many God–called evangelists who are truly
evangelists because most evangelists today are
really just stirring up people in the church. True
evangelists can't live without getting people into
the body of Christ. The office of an evangelist
gathers people to Jesus, and usually the evangelist in the church is someone that might even
annoy us. It could be that little old lady who

brings all the kids to church, and they are all noisy. The heart of an evangelist always thinks about outreach and how he can attract people to Jesus.

I believe pastors *guard*. The office of a pastor is protective. It is the heart of a shepherd. A pastor is a father of a flock of people. They watch over a congregation with a desire to meet their needs and to protect the church. Finally, I believe teachers *ground*. They want to teach precepts from God's Word so that we don't fall off cliffs. Teachers keep us from making the same mistake twice because they instill knowledge to God's people. A teacher will attach what we do to the Bible, and they impart the Scripture in a way that everyone can understand.

Rob: So apostles govern, prophets guide, evangelists gather, pastors guard, and teachers ground. That's an excellent description of the primary mission of each of these God–called offices. We've been trying to lay all of those things on the pastor.

Dan: I think it takes all of us, Rob. All of these offices are essential to God's Church.

Rob: Absolutely! We've got to seek the Lord on how to start operating in a fivefold, Dan, or we'll continue to over burden pastors. And I think this is going to be a challenge for those in denomina-tional churches like the Church of the Nazarene.

Dan: What I have found in my travels are churches in the "Nazarene kingdom" that have been plagued with past issues like legalism, tra-ditionalism, or worship wars. Their world is no bigger than that. They are so set in their ways that it's difficult for the Holy Spirit to break in. These churches will have a hard time adjusting to an apostolic model of a fivefold. Then I go to other churches that aren't encumbered by past problems—issues from the past and tradition-alism. These churches aren't old wine skins, but they are trying to become new wine skins. And because they aren't encumbered by anything, they are filled with expectancy for the future. They anticipate what the Holy Spirit is going to do. I truly believe that in the coming days the churches that will be thriving will not be the ones that draw people to an organized church with predicable services, but what will draw people is an authentic kingdom experience where the Spirit is free to move.

Rob: Yes, and that kingdom experience will be established through a fivefold.

Dan: I also believe that people are going to be drawn to spiritual fathers and not denominations. People are going to be drawn to those who are operating in the offices the Spirit has established. The Bible says that God appoints apostles and prophets. People don't appoint them, but God appoints them. I think the Church can have the five offices and not pay them because God is the one that appoints them and not a pastor or church board. But I really don't know how we can institute this in the Nazarene world. I really don't.

I guess I would say this: there are a lot of district superintendents who are good friends of mine, and my prayer is that the district superintendents wouldn't just be the CEOs who solve the problems, fix the messes, and fill the pulpits, but my prayer is that they would seek the Lord to see if they are apostles who could give away the anointing to their pastors. If our denomination would think about moving apostles into the position of a district superintendent, then, every time they were around their pastors, their pastors would leave with a greater fire and anointing because they would receive an impartation from their district superintendent functioning as apostles. That is my prayer for the Nazarene church. I want to see us become a kingdom government instead of a government of man.

Rob: Don't you think that is what Paul meant when he said, "For if you were to have countless tutors in Christ, yet you would not have many fathers" (1 Corinthians 4:15a).

Dan: Yes, I do.

Rob: An apostolic father will give birth to future generations because of the anointing that they carry. It is a different mindset or way of thinking. We are used to teachers, but we need spiritual fathers. Like you said, people will be drawn to fathers. In fact, I believe that until we start to recognize apostolic fathers, we will continue to have spiritual orphans in the Church. Dan, I know this is going to be difficult in our tribe to make the transition, but how do we incorporate apostles and prophets? We gladly recognize evangelists, pastors, and teachers, but how do we start to recognize apostles and prophets? I realize that they are God–called, but what can a local pastor do?

Dan: That is a hard question for me to answer. From my perspective, I'm just a layman. I'm not an ordained elder. I'm just a person that God called to wake up the Church, and He opened up doors for me to do it. I will say this: there are hundreds of pastors who consider me an apostle or a father, and that's probably because of the call of God in my life.

Rob: Yes, I believe you are a spiritual father to many people.

Dan: At least I'm someone who tries to pray a blessing and an anointing over pastors. I just believe there has to be a total paradigm shift in our thinking. I think we need to stop trying to do ministry with our best efforts, with our best strategy, with our best planning, and just get back to the simplicity of the primitive New Testament Church that was Spirit led and Spirit driven. I think if we would become a presence-driven church instead of a program-driven church, the presence of God would enable us to function the way we should.

If we were really following the cloud of the presence of God, then we wouldn't have to teach people to go reach the lost, to multiply churches, to deliver people from oppression, or to pray for the sick. Those kinds of activities would flow out of living in the manifest presence of Jesus, and Jesus doesn't want anyone to be lost. He wants all to be saved, touched, healed, and restored in our cities. But when the Church becomes an institution led by the efforts of people, it will always hit and miss its mission. All of this is going to take a massive paradigm shift, Rob. The whole purpose of a fivefold is to equip the people to do the works of ministry. The five offices aren't supposed to do the works of ministry, but the body of Christ is. The saints are to do the works, and they will all do extraordinary works if they are being equipped by the fivefold.

Rob: There you go!

Dan: Honestly, I believe the only way we will start to recognize apostles and prophets is to admit that we don't have the answers. We're going to have to admit that only God has the answers, and, therefore, we need the kingdom of God to invade our kingdom. It starts with repentance! Jesus began His ministry that way. He told people to repent because the kingdom of God was near (see Matthew 4:17). So, I believe if we are going to operate in a kingdom mindset, then the first step will be repentance. I hear rumblings of that from our leaders. I hear them speaking about that from time to time and read it on the Internet or in e–mails. I hear our leaders calling us to repent for a greater manifestation of the glory. I think that is the only hope.

Rob: I agree!

Dan: We cannot be reactionary, but we need to bring reformation. The kingdom of God is strong enough to bring about the reformation that we need. We must allow the kingdom of God and His government to be the kingdom we operate under because the only thing that is going to remain is His kingdom. The Scripture says His kingdom won't end (see Luke 1:33). Denominations won't remain, but the kingdom of God will remain forever. His kingdom will reform everything that we do and everything that we are.

Rob: So true. The kingdom of God should be our only heavenly model for ministry. Unfortunately, we have had business models of government in the Church, so I agree that we must repent for imposing man's structure on the Church and receive the kingdom of God with its governmental style. And the kingdom of God will bring with it an apostolic fivefold. It would be what God established. He has called apostles, prophets, evangelists, pastors, and teachers to lead and equip the Church. I really believe that there are modern-day apostles and prophets. I do not believe that they have all died. The original apostles obviously have all died, but I believe that God is still calling apostles and prophets, don't you?

Dan: Yes, I do. There are a lot of views in the Church that are based on cessationism (the doctrine that revelatory and miraculous spiritual gifts passed away when all the apostles died, and, therefore, there are no more apostles and prophets functioning in the supernatural). People have developed a theology that thinks if a person didn't see Jesus alive or wasn't personally called by Him like the disciples, then they can't be an apostle. That is not the case in the Bible, and I always go back to the Bible.

The Bible identifies the twelve apostles and the seventy who were sent (see Luke 10:1), but Matthias was chosen after Jesus had died, which would make thirteen plus the seventy. And then add Paul. He was an apostle. There are actually over ninety apostles in the Bible, including people like Apollos, Barnabas, Andronicus, Junia, Titus, and Timothy. Some of these apostles never saw Jesus before His crucifixion, but they were God–called apostles.

Rob: And one of them was probably a woman, too. You mentioned Junia in Romans 16:7.

Dan: I think apostles are present today, but I think a lot of times that they aren't understood. People in our tribe aren't trained to recognize them, but God still appoints apostles today. And when God appoints someone, no man can shut that appointment down.

I also believe that there are still God-called prophets. Certainly, I would agree that there is a lot of flakiness that goes on from self-proclaimed prophets, but the ones who have been ordained by God speak words that lead people into greater revelations of who Jesus is. The spirit of prophecy is just the testimony of Jesus as it says in Revelation 19:10, so true prophets guide leadership into a more intimate relationship with Jesus. And that's the call to this generation! We need to become the bride of Christ who is intimately intertwined with the Groom and coming King.

Rob: Let's tease this out a bit more. Apostles, prophets, evangelists, pastors, and teachers are called by God and not appointed by man. So these offices often bypass the ecclesiastical protocol. In other words, God appoints people that we wouldn't, and therefore, we overlook or fail to recognize God's man or woman. We're not able to recognize the anointing on someone because they didn't pass through our denominational system to receive man's ordination. Should we talk about that?

M-11 (Mission 2011, Nazarene Mission Conference) is the perfect example, Dan. You are a layman, and you have never been formally trained. You don't have a license to preach, and you never graduated from a Bible college or seminary. In fact, you were a carpenter, but you have a divine call on your life. At M-11, a conference with more than three thousand people in attendance, that call was recognized because you were asked to preach, and there was an incredible anointing that fell on us as you spoke. Yet, if we are locked into paradigms or wine skins of ecclesiastical structures, we are going to bypass the anointing that you or others like you carry. We will fail to recognize the mantle God has placed on someone because they aren't "part of the system." Is that right?

Dan: Yes, that is right. Let me just share about M-11. I was a year and half into this itinerant ministry and had already been to a lot of districts. Many district superintendents had called the Global Ministry Center (Church of the Nazarene Headquarters) and told them that I should speak at M-11. I am a layman and was just a year and half into this ministry, but God was doing extraordinary things in my meetings. So I was asked to speak at our national missions conference. I truly was afraid and nervous—I mean I was petrified! But there were literally dozens of district superintendents who sent me e-mails and texts saying that they had their districts praying and fasting for an outpouring of the Holy Spirit at that conference.

When I went into the conference, I was just so overwhelmed with the feeling of what God wanted to do. I truly believed that God wanted to birth a kingdom movement in the Church of the Nazarene to where we would operate in such power that our cities and nation would be transformed by Christ. I felt great anticipation and all this excitement, yet I was burdened because I didn't want to do anything except what God wanted to do. In fact, the night before we met in a hotel room at the Galt House. There were about forty people crammed into a room where we prayed for three hours. We were certain that God was going to come.

When I stood up and started preaching the next day, I felt like I had all these prayers supporting me. I didn't even take my Bible on stage because God told me to trust Him. I don't even know to this day what I preached—I never listened or watched it, but I do remember that during the message people started coming forward around the front. They fell on their faces and started crying out.

Rob: That's true. I was there.

Dan: I believe God told me to lay hands on people after the message. There have been hundreds of testimonies from people who were healed that day. There were so many people who came through that line for an impartation, and I didn't even know at the time what impartations were. We were all overwhelmed by the manifest presence of Jesus, but as soon as that service was over, controversy and criticism surfaced. People started attacking me and the service, and I had no idea how something like that could have happened when the presence of God was so weighty.

Rob, you are a graduate of Mount Vernon Nazarene University and Nazarene Theological Seminary, and you have your doctorate from United Theological Seminary. You have been a pastor/minister for over thirty years. Can you tell me from your perspective what happened after that service? How could there be so much controversy after the glory of God came like it did?

Rob: I believe the answer is in the failure to recognize the apostolic anointing. From my perspective, we have such a limited paradigm of ministry in our minds that we're unable to sense an authentic outpouring of the Holy Spirit. You mentioned the wine skins in Luke 5. Our wine skins are so small that we can't really see how God can use someone like you, and often God will come through vessels that provoke our limited perspectives.

What I believe happened at M-11 is that people were offended with you because you're a layman and they didn't believe that you had the authority to lay hands on people and pray for an impartation. You are a guy that hasn't had formal training, yet God has chosen to use you and call you to this ministry. So, since you are asking, I believe that some of the controversy arose out of those who did not recognize the anointing because it came through a vessel that people least expected. What's so sad to me is that God used an apostle to usher in the glory of God to bring about a corporate shift in our movement, but people missed the opportunity because they were too distracted by religious perspectives.

I believe if we are going to open up to a biblical model, an apostolic fivefold, if we are going to open up to this type of ministry, then it is going to take humility across the body of Christ to recognize that sometimes the number of degrees behind a minister's name doesn't matter. My education doesn't qualify me. Jesus does. I'm glad for my education and I don't scorn the opportunities that I've had, but academics cannot overshadow the anointing. A calling and anointing from God supersedes anything, and if that is missed, then we will overlook and misjudge extraordinary moves of the Holy Spirit.

Dan: I believe that, Rob. And I have nothing against a formal education, either.

Rob: Same here. I'm not suggesting that a person shouldn't have to go through training if they are called into the ministry. But the point I'm making is that God chose to use you *without* formal training. He called you to wake up churches and to reform movements. So if people don't allow their thinking to expand to accept the anointing on apostolic leaders, even those leaders who haven't been academically trained, then we'll keep failing to recognize those moments when the Holy Spirit desires to bring a corporate shift in our movement through those people.

As I observed M-11, I believe that was a time when God answered our prayers. I believe that was a moment when God gave us an opportunity as a movement and as a denomination to make a shift. Many people were touched by God including me. Many people were healed, delivered, set free, experienced a fresh baptism, and received calls for ministry. But there were a few, unfortunately, that didn't recognize the move of the Holy Spirit. They were too focused on other things. They were looking at the instrument and not looking to Jesus. They failed to see the presence of God that day. So, frankly, we need to humble ourselves and repent.

Dan: I agree.

Rob: Most people reading this realize the statistics of our tribe. The Church of the Nazarene is suffering in the United States. We are not a growing church, and this is true of many other mainline denominations. There are no easy answers, I admit, but I believe that we need to look at the Bible to create biblical models and biblical paradigms for our churches. Is there anything else that you want to add to this before we move on?

Dan: I just have a longing to see us functioning as the body of Christ where we go from glory to glory and do not grow weary in well doing. I believe that if we keep pursuing His presence and if we remain in a place of intimacy with Jesus, no matter what the enemy throws at us, we will keep our peace and joy. I believe the fivefold is a biblical government that propagates intimacy with Jesus. Those offices equip us to be spiritually healthy.

I believe that we need to experience sonship/ daughtership and know that God is our Father and that we are members of a royal family. Apostolic leadership can help to establish that. It can help to establish the assurance and confidence that we are part of a family and that we don't have to live as spiritual orphans. We are more than conquerors. I honestly don't know who can make this work, but if the first-century church did, then we can do it again.

Rob: Amen.

I remember the day when I sat alone at the park, a place where I often go to spend time with Jesus, and I had my Bible open to Ephesians chapter four. As I sat there, the presence of God seemed to swell. His weighty presence filled my car. I read Ephesians 4:11–16 with new revelation and insight. I want to conclude this chapter by unfolding the insight God gave me that day. Here's the passage:

> And He gave some *as* apostles, and some *as* prophets, and some *as* evangelists, and some *as* pastors and teachers, for the equipping of the saints for the work of service, to the building up of the body of Christ; until we all attain the unity of the faith, and of the knowledge of the Son of God, to a mature man, to the measure of the stature which belong to the fullness of Christ. As a result, we are no longer to be children, tossed here and there by waves and carried about by every wind of doctrine, by the trickery of men, by craftiness in deceitful scheming; but speaking the truth in love, we are to grow up in all *aspects* into Him who is the head, *even* Christ, from whom the whole body, being fitted and held together by what every joint supplies, according to the proper working of each individual part, causes the growth of the body for the building up of itself in love (Ephesians 4:11–16).

I noticed that the end result or product of equipped saints was the "building up of the body of Christ" (Ephesians 4:12). I asked myself, "What does the body of Christ look like when it is built up?" The following verses answered that question. In fact, there are five characteristics that are observable.

Unity: Paul wrote, "Until we all attain the unity of the faith" (Ephesians 4:13). In this same chapter Paul exhorted us to "preserve the unity of the Spirit" (v. 3). There is a tremendous need for the body of Christ to be unified. The possibilities are unlimited when a group of believers are unified in the Spirit. God looked at His people in Genesis and noted, "They are one people, and they all have the same language . . . nothing which they purpose to do will be impossible for them" (Genesis 11:6). Unfortunately, their motives were self-centered and so God confused their language, but the point remains that because of their unity, they could have accomplished anything. Take notice of the believers in the book of Acts. Because they were "all with one mind," they persevered and prevailed. Unity is vital to the ongoing mission of the Church, and without it we will never fulfill the mandates God has given to us.

Maturity: Paul continued in the same verse, "To a mature man, to the measure of the stature which belongs to the fullness of Christ" (Ephesians 4:13b). Spiritual immaturity has plagued the Church for years. In one church Paul was unable to address them as spiritual adults, but he dumbed down his message because they were like spiritual infants (see 1 Corinthians 3:1–3). Their immaturity manifested through jealousy and strife. They were acting as people completely in the flesh and not in the Spirit. There are carnal, self-centered people in churches today who whine, complain, throw fits, and when they are unable to get their own way, they leave the church because of offense. We cannot build the Church with immature believers. We must "press on to the maturity" (Hebrews 6:1).

Stability: The next verse says, "As a result, we are no longer to be children, tossed here and there by waves and carried about by every wind of doctrine" (Ephesians 4:14a). These days believers are in and out, up and down, hot and cold, or fired up and fizzled out. Much of this instability is due to ignorance of the Word. Think about the subject matter of this book, even this chapter, and how it stretches the institutional paradigms we've been reared in. Our understanding of the Bible is too often limited to wine skins that have been contrived to fit our denominational churches.

Add to that, we've been fed with shallow devotionals and sermons that haven't plumbed the depths of God's Word. We know little about how to function in a culture of the kingdom. Consequently, people are tossed by this or that, and without an apostolic environment, we only perpetuate our spiritual ignorance. We must have stable believers. We must have congregations made up of stable Christians who aren't easily enticed by the craftiness of man's schemes. We need apostolically equipped believers who will persevere until revival affects our churches and cities.

Charity: Paul continued, "But speaking the truth in love, we are to grow up in all aspects into Him who is the head, even Christ" (Ephesians 4:15). According to this verse, we are to grow up in all things, but that is accomplished when the truth is made known in the context of love (*agape*). "Love never fails. . . ." (1 Corinthians 13:8). If we are immersed in an atmosphere of love, we are in the presence of God because He *is* love (1 John 4:8). In that kind of environment, we will disclose the truth. We will speak truth to one another. Literally, this means "truthing the truth" or forging the truth.

Authentic love creates a heavenly atmosphere, and when heaven invades earth, God's truths will be made known. When that happens, Paul said that we will grow up (*auxano*), which means to increase and to expand in the things of God. This is desperately needed in our churches. We've got to remove the masks and declare the whole purpose of God (see Acts 20:27), or else we will fail to grow up into Him who is the head.

Efficiency: Paul concluded, "From whom the whole body, being fitted and held together by what every joint supplies, according to the proper working of each individual part, causes the growth of the body" (Ephesians 4:16). All the parts of the body of Christ are doing what they are supposed to do. Think of that! No one is standing around wondering what their responsibility is; the parts of the body are equipped and assigned, and, as a result, there is growth in the body. This is a picture of an efficient church — a healthy body.

I remember writing these five words on a tablet while sitting in my car: unity, maturity, stability, charity, and efficiency. Those are five characteristics of the body of Christ that has been properly edified. Then I asked myself a series of questions from Ephesians 4:11–12 that I want to walk through with you. First, how does the body of Christ experience those five characteristics that just listed from verses 13–16? The answer is when the body of Christ is built up. Second, how is the body of Christ built up? The answer is by the saints who do the work of service. Third, how do we get the saints to do work of service? The answer is they must be equipped. Fourth, how will the saints be adequately equipped? Christ has the answer. He gave apostles, prophets, evangelists, pastors, and teachers to equip the saints so that they'll do the work of service for the building up of the body of Christ, and a fully edified body will manifest those five characteristics. This is a biblical model that we can't improve upon. An apostolic culture will produce a healthy church.

I agree with Dan. There are no easy answers for transitioning our churches into an apostolic fivefold. But we've got to try! We've got to ask the Holy Spirit for wisdom and revelation on how to implement this in our churches and movements. We must ask God to call apostles and prophets just as much as we seek Him for pastors, teachers, and evangelists. We must think about apostolic training in our Christian schools and not just pastoral training. Perhaps we're coercing God–called prophets or apostles into the mold of a pastor because we're limited in our thinking. The bottom line is God still calls apostles and prophets, and we need to seek the Lord on how we can function with them.

Chapter Seven

WHAT HINDERS REVIVAL

Born in 1907 in the city of Leeds, in Yorkshire, England, Leonard Ravenhill became one of England's foremost traveling evangelists. He not only was used mightily in England, but his ministry of preaching and writing has continued to provoke and challenge the present day Church. Ravenhill's assessment of the American church was quite grim. He likened the Church to a sleeping sentry because after being charged with the task of guarding our citadels, we fell asleep on the wall.

I had the privilege of hearing him speak, and his message was as convicting as his books. He described a vision he had of large billows of smoke rising from the earth into the heavens but contrasted that with a small wisp of smoke rising to the heavens. The Holy Spirit spoke to Ravenhill and said, "The large billows of smoke represent the amount of sin, immorality, and iniquity that is rising up from the earth. The small wisp of smoke is the amount of intercession being lifted to the heavens by the Church." It's little wonder then that the enemy has crept into our cities, churches, families, and homes. I'm reminded of

Paul's words, "Awake, sleeper, And arise from the dead, And Christ will shine on you" (Ephesians 5:14).

A few years before Ravenhill's death, I watched an interview with this great revivalist. He was asked the question: Why don't we see revival in our nation? His immediate response was stated with no hesitation. He quoted Jeremiah, "For My people have committed two evils; They have forsaken Me, the fountain of living waters, And hewn themselves cisterns — broken cisterns that can hold no water" (Jeremiah 2:13 NKJV). "America has turned her back on God," Ravenhill said.

He went on to explain that there is no other water source. God is the only living water that will quench our thirst. He also described how we have developed man–made strategies that are likened to broken cisterns, and they'll never hold water. They'll never carry the blessing. Much like David when he tried to transport the Ark on a man–made cart, human strategies always fail. That is why the Church of America has failed time and time again according to Ravenhill. Our only hope, he lamented, is brokenness, repentance, and a sincere turning back to God.

I desperately desire to experience revival in my church, city, and nation. I want to see citywide transformation across our country. I'm encouraged by the stories I've heard from Rhonda Hughey, the author of *Desperate for His Presence*. Several leaders, including Rhonda, gathered for breakfast this past Christmas season. Sitting across the table from her, I listened as she told of ongoing revivals not just in other countries but in the United States, too. So as we lament for *more* of His presence, His presence is breaking out from coast to coast. Yet, as I celebrate the victories, my heart still breaks for those churches that seem cold and dead. Revival is being hindered in many churches, denominations, and movements. There are reasons for that hindrance, and this chapter will discuss some of them.

Dan has given nearly seven years of his life to the task of waking up the Church. He is in different churches and different denominations almost every week of the year. There are churches he enters that have yielded to the leadership of the Holy Spirit, and they are being used by God to touch their city for Christ. However, that is not the story with many other churches — in fact, *too* many. So I wanted to talk with him, from his perspective, about the subject of revival and what hinders it. In some ways, this chapter echoes the cries of Ravenhill and others like him. I believe this is an up to date perspective not only on factors that hinder revival but also what can be done to usher in His presence with lasting fruit.

Rob: One of the first books that I ever read after I was born again was *Why Revival Tarries* by Leonard Ravenhill. I'm sure that you've read this book and were touched as Ravenhill addressed reasons why America hasn't experienced a true revival. I read this book in 1982, and I believe our nation still hasn't experienced a mighty outpouring. We've had significant outpourings — some have even lasted for several years, but the average church hasn't experienced a true revival — one that transforms the church and the city around it. My question to you is, why? What are the problems that you can identify in the average church that hinders revival? What are some of the more pressing issues that churches are facing?

Dan: Well, obviously sin and carnality. The fact remains that people aren't totally consecrated to God—I mean totally dead to sin and alive in Him. That, in my opinion, is the number one hindrance. I actually believe that there are a lot of people who don't even know what revival is. The reason for that is many people in our churches don't have an awareness of what a greater move of God looks like because it's been so long since there's been a mighty outpouring. People don't know what they're missing because it has been absent for so long. So I think there is a lot of ignorance about what a true revival might look like. This ignorance also leads to fear because when God starts to pour out His Spirit on a church, people are unaware of what God is doing and it causes them to be afraid. People have read or heard things about revival, but it's usually been written by people who haven't experienced an authentic move of God.

So if I was making a list of what hinders revival, I would start with sin. When we are unwilling to get rid of sin, it will always block a move of God. Second would be carnality. If people aren't willing to completely die to themselves and allow God to cleanse their heart from the essence of sin, then revival will never last. Third is ignorance— ignorance of God's Word, the things of the Spirit, the kingdom of God, or the aspects of an outpouring. Finally, because there is so much ignorance in the Church, it leads to fear. Fear always prevents a move of God.

Rob: Yes, I preached a message one time called "The Three Impediments." It dealt with the three biggest reasons why there isn't breakthrough in people's lives. The impediments are sin, fear, and unbelief.

Dan: Unbelief always hinders a great move of God. When Jesus came to His own town of Nazareth, it says, "And He could do no miracles there. . . . and He wondered at their unbelief" (Mark 6:5–6). But in some ways all of these things are symptoms. I believe the main reason that revival tarries is because of the lack of a tangible manifest presence of the glory of God that moves upon people. That move will only come when His people get desperate, cry out, and repent. Without repentance, brokenness, desperate prayer, and radical obedience, revival will just be a topic. It will not be a reality. That being said, I do see pockets of revival springing up around the country and around the world where people are desperate for God.

Rob: Yes, I agree. But it's always preceded by hunger and desperation, isn't it?

Dan: Without a doubt. We must be hungry and desperate for deeper encounters with God or else we're wasting our time even talking about revival. Encounters with God create a desire in us for others to experience encounters. Encounters make us hungry for others around us to experience what we have. But it starts with us, Rob. We must be so desperate for Jesus. We must be willing to cry out, pray, and believe for a mighty outpouring that transforms us, our churches, our cities, and the world around us. Therefore, I believe revival tarries because people are self–satisfied. They aren't desperate and hungry for God.

Rob: I agree, Dan. You touched on this, but I want to come back to it. Often when God *does* move, He comes in ways we aren't expecting, isn't that true?

Dan: Oh, yeah! God can't be put into a box or paradigm that fits every church. When He comes,

He comes His own way, and if we're not sensitive to the Holy Spirit, we will push Him away when He comes.

Rob: I believe one of the first messages I ever heard you teach addressed this issue of sensitivity to the Spirit. A friend gave me a CD of one of your messages, but I hadn't met you yet. I sat in the parking lot of a restaurant, with tears running down my face, as I listened to the message you preached. You talked about improper ways we can treat the Holy Spirit. I want you to talk about that now. I believe God comes like new wine, but because we're used to an old wine skin, we mistreat the Spirit. We reject the new wine that He is pouring out. We say, "Come, Holy Spirit; we need you," but when He comes, we push Him out the door. So let's talk about that for a moment. What are some of the biblical ways we mistreat the Holy Spirit? Go back to that message you preached. What are the ways we mistreat the Spirit when He comes?

Dan: First, we can blaspheme the Holy Spirit (Matthew 12:31). This is what the Pharisees did when Jesus cast a demon out of someone. Jesus told them that the kingdom of God had come upon them because He was casting demons out. When the kingdom comes, so does the Spirit of God, but the Pharisees were unable to recognize the Spirit of God and the nature of the kingdom. Consequently, they spoke against the Spirit. I believe there are people today who speak against the move of God because they can't recognize the activities of the kingdom when it comes. It's very dangerous to speak against the Spirit of God because there's no greater manifestation of God. The Holy Spirit is the promise of the Father (see Luke 24:49). Blasphemy speaks against that promise.

Second, we can lie to the Holy Spirit (Acts 5:3). Ananias lied to the Spirit and tried to be something that he wasn't. He acted generously when in reality he was stingy. I believe that when the Holy Spirit comes we need to be real. We need to be honest and repent. I believe that if we try to act spiritual in the presence of God, we are lying to the Holy Spirit.

In the same passage, we learn thirdly that we can test the Spirit (Acts 5:9). Ananias' wife went along with the lie, and she perpetuated the sin of her husband. I believe that if we're in a church where there are no miracles, growth, transformations, or salvations, we need to come to the conclusion that the Spirit of God probably isn't moving. And if we don't come to that fact and get real and repent, then we are perpetuating that lie. We are part of the ongoing problem and not the solution. What is worse, though, is that there are serious consequences for lying and testing the Spirit.

Rob: Wow, Dan. That is sobering to me. It's like the greater the increase of the Spirit upon us the greater the consequences for working against the Spirit.

Dan: It's true. God's judgement intensifies when His Spirit magnifies. Asking for His presence can be a blessing, but if we're not serious about repenting when His Spirit moves upon us, it can reap some serious consequences.

The fourth way we can mistreat the Holy Spirit is by resisting Him. I think about Stephen's message when he was quoting the history of God's people in Acts 7:51: "You men who are stiff-necked and uncircumcised in heart and ears are always resisting the Holy Spirit; you are doing just as your fathers did." There have been many times when the Holy Spirit tries to break in, but if we don't totally yield to Him, then we are resisting the Holy Spirit. Resisting the Holy Spirit can be evident in many ways such as: resisting Him in repentance, resisting His call, resisting

His leading or prompting, or resisting Him from having total preeminence in your life. You can just resist or push back the Holy Spirit because you are stubborn and stiff–necked. I will tell you that He is a person, and He can be pushed back often enough to where He won't continue to strive with us. We can resist Him to the point that He won't press Himself on us any longer. We should not resist the Holy Spirit.

The fifth way that we can mistreat the Holy Spirit is by grieving Him (Ephesians 4:30). We can grieve the Spirit when we gossip about people, lie, fail to tithe and give resources to God, or let unwholesome words come out of our mouths. I think grieving the Holy Spirit happens all the time in the Church when we claim to be Spirit–filled, yet everything but the Spirit comes out of our mouths when we're talking. This grieves the Holy Spirit. It saddens Him. He is a person, He has feelings, He is the Comforter, He is the Helper, He is the Healer, He is the Sustainer, He is the Provider, He has emotions, He feels, and He is the Spirit of God. We can grieve Him.

The sixth way that we can mistreat the Spirit is by rejecting Him (1 Thessalonians 4:8). When we reject God's message of sanctification, Paul says that we're not rejecting man but God who gives

His Holy Spirit to us. The Spirit of God sanctifies our hearts. He cleanses and purifies us just like Peter said when the Spirit fell on them (Acts 15:8–9). To reject sanctification is to reject the Spirit who sanctifies.

Rob: That's why the old–timers used to preach "holiness or hell."

Dan: Very true. God desires a holy people, Rob. He will call us all to be sanctified. The Bible says, "Faithful is He who calls you" (1 Thessalonians 5:24). When we reject His call to be sanctified, that is disobedience and that is a serious issue with God.

Seventh, we can insult the Holy Spirit (Hebrews 10:29). When we trample the blood of Jesus, the blood of the new covenant that sanctifies, we are insulting the Spirit. We are treating something that is very significant to God as unimportant. When He comes into our churches, He comes to purify and sanctify. If we compromise and are not obedient to the work He desires to do, then it's like putting Jesus on the cross all over again and insulting the Spirit of grace.

The eighth and final way we can mistreat the Holy Spirit is by quenching Him (1 Thessalonians

5:19). To quench the Holy Spirit means to suppress or choke His influence in our lives. Some scholars define quenching as putting a blanket on a fire. If you keep placing blankets over a fire, it will eventually snuff a fire completely out. Rob, we've been talking about this recently.

Rob: Yes, we have. And usually when we quench the Spirit, we also despise prophetic utterances as Paul went on to write (1 Thessalonians 5:20). That simply means that we treat prophetic words with contempt. In other words, prophetic words aren't important to us. We give little credence to them in our gatherings. Think about it Dan, how many of our churches are prophetic cultures where the Spirit of God speaks through His people in such a manner that we receive edification, exhortation, and consolation (see 1 Corinthians 14:3)? I would answer not many. So if we're quenching the Spirit, we are also shutting down the prophetic voices.

Dan: A number of terrible things occur when we quench the Holy Spirit. The Spirit is the one who leads us into all truth, so if we quench the Spirit, how will we receive truth (see John 16:13)? The Spirit is the one that brings conviction (see John 16:8), so if we quench the Spirit, we won't sense the need to repent of sin. The Holy Spirit is the one who gives revelation, information, illumination, words of knowledge, supernatural gifts, and guides us through difficult seasons in our lives. If we quench the Spirit's influence in our lives, then we have suppressed all of these blessings. If we quench the Spirit, then we will be spiritually lost because we will suppress the Spirit's guidance.

All the way through Scripture we learn that the Spirit is the one who sanctifies us and the Spirit is the one that gives us new birth, but if we quench the Spirit, we are suppressing our possibilities of being redeemed. We can quench the Spirit by not praying continually, by griping instead of thanking God, by complaining instead of worshipping, by pushing people out who have prophetic words instead of testing everything out to find the good, or by becoming judges and sitting in the seat of scoffers like Pharisees. When we quench the Spirit like the Pharisees did, we don't even recognize the visitation of the Spirit because we are so busy being "watch dogs." There are so many things that can happen when we quench the Spirit.

Quenching the Spirit is a major reason that we don't see revival. There are subtle ways we can quench the Spirit, too. I think about how Peter was compromising by acting in one manner around the Jews and then in another manner around the Gentiles in Galatians 2. Let me add, this occurred after he was sanctified. We must pay careful attention that nothing springs up in our hearts after we've been purified (see Hebrews 12:15). Peter was manipulating the Spirit. He was living a lie. When we act one way at church and then another way at home or work, we're manipulating the Spirit, and this will prevent Him from working in our lives. It's another way we can quench the Spirit. There are many ways we push the Spirit out, but I believe that revival can only come if we are willing to welcome the Holy Spirit any way He desires to come.

I know that He is drawn to a broken and contrite heart. He will not despise that kind of person. The Bible says, "The sacrifices of God are a broken spirit; a broken and a contrite heart, O God, You will not despise" (Psalm 51:17). Isaiah 57:15 says, "For thus says the high and exalted One Who lives forever, whose name is Holy, 'I dwell *on* a high and holy place, and *also* with the contrite and lowly of spirit in order to revive the spirit of the lowly and to revive the heart of the contrite.'" I think we need to lower ourselves in humility, repentance, and desperation, and then cry out because I believe that God wants to bring revival more than we ever want it. I know that sounds simple, but I just believe that we have to get desperate and cry out until the awakening of

God comes back to our church and revival breaks out in our cities. And maybe then the kingdom of God could come, and His will be done on earth as it is in heaven.

Rob: Yes! I agree with that. You know, I remember hearing that message of how we mistreat the Holy Spirit, and I just wept, Dan. I was a mess. There have been times in services where the Holy Spirit wanted to move, and we have pushed Him out the door. I don't ever want to do that personally, and I don't want to do that corporately, either. When the Holy Spirit comes to me, it might be awkward to say, do, or confess something, but I just don't want to grieve, quench, resist, or shut down the Holy Spirit in any way.

As you were talking I was thinking about Matthew chapter twelve where the Pharisees were not able to discern the works of the Holy Spirit. Jesus had cast out a demon, and the Pharisees were blaming it on Beelzebub, the prince of demons. Think about what Jesus said in this passage. The following is my paraphrase of Jesus' words: "If I cast out a demon, it is because the kingdom has come, but you guys can't discern the kingdom. You guys can't discern the work of the Spirit, which is a manifestation of my kingdom coming. You guys actually attribute the work of the Spirit to the work of the enemy." I don't want to do that, Dan.

Yet, what breaks my heart is that people in our churches and in our tribe cannot discern the work of the Holy Spirit. I have been doing some extensive teaching on 1 Thessalonians chapter five about quenching the Spirit, where it talks about testing everything (see 1 Thessalonians 5:21). I think people use that verse as an excuse to be critical about the functions of the Holy Spirit. As I studied that verse, the point of examining everything is not to become a critic, but rather it is to find the good and to cling to it.

Dan: I agree. Usually when the Holy Spirit is being poured out, there will be things we have to examine in order to see if they are real or not. But we have to disregard the unreal and hold tightly to what *is* real.

Rob: Exactly. I made the statement one time that during outpourings and moves of God in revivals, there will be inauthentic and immature manifestations from people. The enemy is always going to try to counterfeit something that is real. You have probably seen that in some of your travels where the enemy attempts to counterfeit something God is doing. But here is the point: If

I'm going to counterfeit money, then I wouldn't counterfeit Monopoly money because it isn't real. It holds no value. I'm only going to counterfeit the real thing. Isn't it true that when you see counterfeit moves of God, the enemy is obviously trying to make a mockery of what is real?

Dan: Yes, absolutely.

Rob: In the midst of the counterfeit, we need to look for the real and authentic and then hold tightly to it rather than just dismissing the whole thing. Too many people have tossed out an actual move of God because they saw something that wasn't real in the midst of it. That is what I believe Paul was saying in 1 Thessalonians 5:21, when he said to hold fast to that which is good. There are too many critics in our churches who, like the Pharisees, can't see the authentic move of God.

Dan: I think we hinder revival by misjudging the Spirit's manifestations, too. Think about how critical people were when the Holy Spirit was poured out at Pentecost.

Rob: Yes, they were mocking the believers for being full of wine (see Acts 2:13). They weren't drunk with wine. They were full of the Holy Spirit. So, I agree. People can even mock the real thing because of their inability to recognize the Holy Spirit. Dan, let's talk about the consequences of rejecting the Holy Spirit. I once heard you preach what you call the "blue verses." It is not a popular message. Talk to us about grieving the Spirit to the point that we will miss His leadings altogether and grieving Him to the point of no return.

Dan: There was a sobering awakening that came to my heart several years ago. During one of my monthly reads through the Bible, God told me to look for His mercy and grace. He wanted me to identify verses dealing with peace and mercy. So I highlighted all those verses in orange because they would represent a safety sign. The next month, I read through the Bible looking for all the wrath, judgment, condemnation, and punishment verses. I highlighted them in blue because I thought sounded like "woe is me." When I looked at the blue verses compared to the orange verses, the wrath verses compared to grace verses, blue verses showed up three and half more times than orange verses. I found in my study that there is a time when God says, "Okay, go ahead and do it your own way." It's never good when God lets go.

I believe it is His will that none should perish, but I also believe that He won't waste grace on those who will continue to trample on it. In Hebrews chapters three and four, there are three verses within a half of page where it says "today" if you hear His voice. What happens if you don't hear His voice anymore? If you can't hear His voice, then you can't come to Him because His voice draws us. We're drawn by the voice of God (see John 6:44). What if we never hear the Spirit again because we have pushed Him out so many times?

If we continue to reject the Holy Spirit, there are two dangers. First, our heart becomes so calloused that we are no longer sensitive to the Spirit. Second, God will stop speaking to us because He knows the end from the beginning, and He knows that you will never respond. I just don't want to ever take a chance with the Holy Spirit and let my heart become hard. So I think it is a serious warning for the Church to always remain obedient, humble, and sensitive to the Holy Spirit. And if we don't understand what the Spirit is doing, then we need to ask Him for revelation (see Ephesians 1:17).

Rob: These "blue verses" are not just in the Old Testament are they?

Dan: No, they are not. I can point out many places in the New Testament where it's a serious sin to reject the Spirit of God. For example, Jesus says if we do not obey Him—His voice or His leadership, we will not see life. Jesus actually says, "The wrath of God abides on him" (John 3:36). So when the Spirit speaks to us, we need to obey, Rob. I don't want God's wrath to dwell on me. We just need to press into the heart of God and become Christlike, Spirit-led, and a Spirit-empowered people.

I believe, more than anything, that we need a greater presence of God in our day so that people can't operate in the flesh and continue grieving and quenching the Spirit. We need an undeniable outpouring of God's Spirit. We need a mighty revival, and I'm praying that people won't question and resist it when it comes. Our world is hanging in the balance and so is the Church. We must not present a watered-down version of the gospel that has no anointing, no conviction, and no persuasion. If we do, then we are causing more harm than good.

Rob: Yes, I agree! You know a verse that is very sobering to me is Matthew 21:43, where Jesus said, "Therefore I say to you, the kingdom of God will be taken away from you and given to a people, producing the fruit of it." That is sobering to me because God is not obligated to any denomination or any group of people. If we aren't producing the fruit of the kingdom, then we'll miss our chance because God will give the kingdom to those who will do something significant for Him. So we need to be obedient to the Holy Spirit and produce kingdom fruit. Revival will come when we remain humble, willing, and not resistant to the works of the Spirit. Amen.

When Jesus discussed putting new wine in old wine skins, He said something that grabs me by the shirt collar. He said, "And no one, after drinking the old wine wishes for new; for he says, 'The old is good enough'" (Luke 5:39). The word "good" (*chrestos*) means useful, better, or more pleasant. It also can mean "more manageable." Wine skins are an analogy for paradigms. They are patterns of thinking or ways of operation. The new wine represents the ways of the Spirit—the fresh revelation and outpouring of Christ.

There is always a problem when God desires to pour out His Spirit in a fresh manner, but we're still operating with a mindset that is old and unfamiliar to the Spirit's *new* movements. What is even worse is when people get used to a certain way in which God has moved and tend to become "experts" of His workings, or so they think. Because human beings are habitual, they start to feel comfortable with their designed programs. They feel at ease when things operate in a manner that they are used to. It becomes "manageable."

I, like Dan, have been to churches where the services are predictable. Pastors and leaders have "managed" the service to the point that they know what will happen each and every minute. And because the congregations have become familiar with that paradigm, they are uncomfortable if or when the Holy Spirit does something "out of the ordinary." If you think about it, all past revivals ended because the recipients of the original outpouring became used to the manner in which God was moving, and when God began moving differently, they rejected the new wine. Thus, the Holy Spirit stopped moving and so did the revival.

The fact is we can never manage the Holy Spirit. He manages us. I've always maintained that one of the greatest hindrances to a move of God was the move of God a week before. When our services come to a close on any given Sunday, it's over. To try to duplicate what God did last Sunday would be disastrous. Every corporate gathering with the body of Christ should function freely in the leadership of the Holy Spirit. This doesn't mean that we can't plan for services, rehearse our music, and prepare our lessons. Being responsible requires preparation; however, we should plan under the direction and scrutiny of the Holy Spirit.

Moreover, in the midst of any gathering, leaders should lead with their ear bent toward heaven. Many times the Holy Spirit has chosen to interrupt our plans and move in ways that we were not expecting. My point is the Holy Spirit manifests for the common good of the Church (see 1 Corinthians 12:7). So I don't want us to be so locked into a mindset of how God manifests that we miss fresh outpourings as history so sadly reveals.

In the early 1900s, a revival known as the Azusa Street Revival occurred and the Pentecostal movement was birthed. Pentecostalism soon became one of the fasting growing movements in the world. By 1908, just two years after the Azusa Street Revival, Pentecostalism had expanded into fifty countries. By 1909, Pentecostalism had spread into China, South Africa, Chile, Argentina, and Brazil. By 1914, this movement had spread rapidly and established its home in every American city.

However, the excitement of this new movement—especially the aspect of speaking in tongues—was not fully embraced by everyone. I'm not suggesting that every manifestation of the Azusa Street Revival was of the Spirit, but many people dismissed the entire event. Leaders in the Holiness movement such as Phineas F. Bresee, founder of the Church of the Nazarene in 1908, spoke out against the growing Pentecostals. Bresee's view of the Azusa Street Revival and its manifestations were noted as having the effect of a "pebble thrown into the sea."[8] Others stated that Pentecostalism was satanic and the last vomit of Satan. By 1919, the Church of the Nazarene dropped the word *Pentecostal* from its name in order to avoid association with those who spoke in tongues. The hardline anti–Pentecostal attitude of many holiness people was summarized in Alma White's 1912 book titled *Demons and Tongues*, "which attributed *glossolalia* (tongues) to demonic influence."[9]

The division between the Pentecostals and those in the non–Pentecostal Holiness movement, including the Church of the Nazarene, was tragic given the fact that both groups had so much in common. While some of the reported manifestations of the Azusa Street revival rightly elicited concern to those within the Holiness movement, the essential conflict centered on the baptism of the Holy Spirit. This was an experience in which both groups strongly believed. The point of disagreement was on the nature of the experience with the Holy Spirit. Stephen Seamands pointed out that those in the Holiness movement argued that the experience was primarily about *purity* (cleansing from a heart divided between self and God), and the Pentecostals believed the experience was about *power* (anointing for ministry and service).[10]

The real tragedy is the lost possible accomplishments had both groups found a common ground upon which to minister together. Frank Billman, a Methodist author and speaker, quoted William DeArteaga when he stated, "What the history of American Christianity would have been like if Methodism had become a Pentecostal denomination in the 1890s can only be imagined."[11] I have often had that same thought concerning the Church of the Nazarene. What could have happened if fear hadn't paralyzed us and dissention hadn't polarized us in the early 1900s? We know what happened to the Methodist denomination. Are the Nazarenes much different today? The reality is that purity and power became separated, a division that impaired both groups (Pentecostals and Nazarenes) to this day, and hindered a revival that some scholars believe could have ushered in a third Great Awakening.

Without the influence of purity, the growing Pentecostals soon lost their emphasis on entire sanctification. By 1910, just four years after the Azusa Street revival, sanctification was essentially denounced by a few people as a second definite work in Pentecostalism, emphasizing instead power for ministry, gifts, and especially speaking in tongues. One author wrote, "The overall effect was to weaken the emphasis on purity within the movement, which arguably weakened the impact of the movement as a whole."[12]

The Holiness movement, including the Church of the Nazarene, steered clear of power in fear of associating with manifestations thought to be emotional and unnecessary. Because we dissociated with those who functioned in the supernatural, our tribe soon lost its understanding of how to function in the extraordinary power and gifting of the Holy Spirit—an issue that Dan and I discussed in chapter two. All would have been stronger had we learned to function in unity in the early 1900s. Instead, we ended up with a plethora of denominations who have built their identity around their own particular distinctive doctrine. Because we've all been divided, our impact has been diluted.

What hinders revival? The answer is sin, fear, ignorance, and an unwillingness to allow the Holy Spirit to create the kind of wine skins that will accommodate what God desires to do. I believe with all my heart that God desires to pour Himself out upon us all. I'm hopeful, and optimistic, that we are going to see a revival in these days that will shake America. But we must be willing to adjust our paradigms. I'm not suggesting that we should become gullible and swallow just anything, but we must be willing to allow the Spirit to move as He desires.

I agree with Dan when he said, "If we don't understand what the Spirit is doing, then we need to ask Him for revelation." Paul prayed that the church in Ephesus would receive a spirit of wisdom and revelation (Ephesians 1:17). Revelation means to remove the veil from our eyes. Revelation is not the creation of new doctrine. It's the exposure of truth that we haven't seen. Revelation should be ongoing, too. We should constantly be growing in revelation and learning new things about God and His kingdom. Let's remain humble and teachable. Equally, we need wisdom to know what to do with the truth that has been given.

In addition to wisdom and revelation, we need to come before God with broken and contrite hearts. Revival will always be hindered by arrogance. Dan underscored the fact that we must come before God with hungry and desperate hearts. We must acknowledge that we're in desperate need for more of His presence in our lives and cities. We might boast that we are rich and have need of nothing, but the truth remains—we are "wretched and miserable and poor and blind and naked" (Revelation 3:17b). The Church in America is in trouble. While we have accomplished some good, we are truly in need of so much more. We may have the reputation of being alive, but in reality we are dead (see Revelation 3:1). It's revival that we need!

Join me in prayer: *God, we hunger for your presence. We desire for you to manifest yourself in greater ways. Create and recreate new wine skins in our hearts and minds that will accommodate your Holy Spirit. We repent of sin, fear, and rebellion. We repent of pushing you away in ignorance. We repent of separating from other brothers and sisters in the faith over minor issues. Revive us again, Oh Lord. We need you, our church needs you, and our cities and nation need you. This we pray in Jesus' name.*

Chapter Eight

SUSTAINING A KINGDOM CULTURE

There are few things that grieve my heart more than when I see or learn of a church that once burned with passion and conviction for the things of God but has lost its fervor. I sympathize with Paul when he wrote to the church in Galatia, "You were running well; who hindered you from obeying the truth?" (Galatians 5:7). I believe that experiencing an encounter with God can almost be detrimental if we're not willing to sustain what we've experienced. If people don't steward and sustain the encounter they've had with God, then they will often become the voice of criticism that mocks the very thing they once experienced. I've witnessed that too many times in my own church. I remember preaching a series of messages that challenged people to move beyond the encounter — to develop a lifestyle that remains in the presence of the Holy Spirit. We never have to leave His presence. The blessing of the New Covenant is that we can *walk* in the Spirit (see Galatians 5:16).

I've taught that there are two kinds of churches: climate churches and culture churches (The same thing applies with individual Christians, too—climate believers and culture believers). Climate churches shift and easily change. Much like weather patterns, climate churches change with every wind of doctrine. Personalities and people shape climate churches, too. So the fervor and spiritual appetite of the church shifts with who comes or who leaves. Culture churches are much different because values are deeply embedded into the lives of those who belong to it. Beliefs and values are embedded into the hearts and lives of the constituency. They are systemic within the body of Christ, and so it doesn't matter who comes or goes. It doesn't matter what happens in our world, politics, nation, or cities. Nothing but the voice of God will shift a culture church.

If we are going to sustain revival, we must have a kingdom culture. As believers we will need to eat, sleep, drink, and breathe kingdom values. They must become embedded into our thinking. Otherwise, we will vacillate up and down. We will be in and out, fired up, and fizzled out, and we'll be unstable in all our ways. This chapter discusses some of those kingdom values and ways we can sustain a revival culture. I believe this chapter will be extremely helpful and practical to believers and churches alike.

Rob: Dan, let's talk about sustaining revival in our churches and in our lives. I believe that it's possible to develop a revival culture or a kingdom culture. Encounters with God are necessary, but we need to sustain the move of God. I remember teaching a series in my church called *Sustaining a Revival Culture*. This series addressed the fact that we can't merely have an event called "revival" over and over again, but we must live "vived" all the time. Corey Jones and I were recently discussing the responsibility of passing a move of God on from one generation to the next and fulfilling the promise of Psalm 145:4 and Isaiah 59:21. There are some ways to sustain a kingdom culture and then pass it on, don't you agree?

Dan: Yes, I do agree. It's essential that we know how to do that, Rob. My heart breaks when I see churches experiencing renewal and then months later I learn that they aren't on fire for God any longer.

Rob: It happens too often.

Dan: I've often joked by saying, "I want to get to the place where I'm no longer needed to bring renewal to the local church." I think it would be great to travel around and simply pour gas on fires that have already been burning.

Rob: I believe that if we're going to sustain a kingdom culture, then one of the essential ingredients is to build alliances with other people who will spur you on.

Dan: We will never sustain revival in isolation. Brothers and sisters must dwell together. There's blessing in unity (see Psalm 133:1–3). We can't burn alone, Rob. It takes others around us to sustain a move of God. You and I have fueled each other for over five years. Our friendship is vital to both of us.

Rob: Yes, I agree. And it's a bit humorous how we first met, too. We talked earlier that when the presence of God began manifesting in my church that I didn't share with too many people except for Kevin Seymour. I'm so thankful for his friendship, but outside of Kevin, I didn't know too many others within the Nazarene tribe whom I could share with. And I'm not sure that I valued strategic alliances up until that time anyway.

Dan: So tell me, what was so humorous about meeting me?

Rob: I'm getting there. I was preaching in Sunbury, Ohio, and when I arrived at the church, I had about an hour before the service began. I called my friend Chuck Millhuff. As we talked, he told me about you and said that we needed to meet. I think I sent a private message on your Facebook explaining the miracles and things that were happening in our church and the prophetic words of knowledge that were happening in our ministry. A few weeks later you called me. That was five years ago on Memorial Day, which was spring of 2010.

Dan: I remember, and we talked for two hours.

Rob: I had asked you to swing by my church on your way to Colorado. You were leaving Pennsylvania and were coming through Columbus, and I wanted to meet you. So on a Thursday morning around 10 a.m., I gathered all my staff and about sixteen of my closest friends from other churches to meet you. Do you remember that?

Dan: Oh yeah! You said that you were a little nervous when you saw me walk in with shorts, sandals, and a button–down shirt. You thought that you were in trouble.

Rob: Absolutely, when I first saw you, nothing that you had on matched! Your goofy gym shorts didn't match your dress shirt, and you had on these old, beat–up sandals. I said to myself, "Oh Lord, what I have I done? All my friends are here, and I've invited a giant clown to speak to us." Of course, you probably looked at me and thought hobbits are for real. Anyways, you sat down for a few moments and after everyone arrived you stood up and spoke for about twenty-five minutes. Five minutes into that talk I was undone. We've been friends ever since that moment. Now I realize the importance of building alliances. I can truly say that we cannot sustain a kingdom culture without building alliances.

Dan: It is not possible, Rob. We have to have comradery and fellowship with other Spirit–filled believers. We have to have brothers and sisters. We have to know that there are other people who function in the Spirit like us. We have to know that we are not alone as we walk in the Spirit. I think the enemy's number one tactic is isolation. There are so many pastors I speak with who are alone. They don't have anyone other than their spouse. It is a tragedy from the enemy, and this aloneness is perpetuated when we operate under a paradigm with an institutional government instead of a kingdom government. An institutional mindset creates abandonment and isolation because it emphasizes personalities and talents instead of the presence of the Holy Spirit, and the Spirit is the unifier. If we operate in a system that squeezes Him out, we will find ourselves alone and isolated from other people.

Rob: Well, we've already discussed that apostles are fathers, but without fathers we will create spiritual orphans.

Dan: The Lord has helped me to bring people together all over this country. There are alliances between believers in all kinds of churches who now communicate, send prayers, words of encouragement, letters, and they frequently talk. There are hundreds of people around this country who know that they are not alone in their pursuit of God, and they are not alone in their desperation for greater things in His kingdom. Hungry people are gathering in churches, living rooms, and offices, crying out together for more of His presence.

Rob: I have friends all over the country now because God has used you to cause that to happen in my life. Let me mention a couple of things that can help build and sustain these strategic alliances. Every Monday morning Corey Jones leads a conference call for about an hour. People can call from across the country, pray, and cry out. I've been on that call and listened to people pray from coast to coast. Corey is anointed to teach and mentor people in prayer, so I would encourage people to get hooked up with that. Along with that, I would also encourage people to attend the Awakening Prayer Conferences that Corey and Beth host every fall.

Dan: Amen. The Prayer Conference is a kingdom event, too. It's larger than just the Nazarene church. It will help people build relationships in an atmosphere of His presence with like–minded people who hunger for the Spirit.

Rob: Also, every Tuesday and Thursday morning you lead a conference call with hundreds of people calling in. This is another opportunity to build and sustain the right kind of friendships. Let me also say that we should be selective who we align ourselves with. The apostle Paul wrote about wrong company corrupting our morals (1 Corinthians 15:33). I want people in my life who will spur me on toward love and good deeds. I like being around those who build my faith and inspire me to chase after the presence of Jesus. The point is God never intended for us to be alone and isolated, so we need to take advantage of opportunities that build community. I heard you say in one of your messages recently that you desire "friends in the cloud." What does that mean?

Dan: To be honest, I really don't have interpersonal communication skills outside of my calling. Even when I speak with strangers, my conversation turns toward Jesus. Because of this call in my life, my conversations with believers are wrapped up in the things of the Spirit. Most of the friends that I have around the country I've met during these last several years in my meetings. Those who are close to me are people that have had encounters in the presence of God with me. We have had breakthroughs together, we have experienced miracles together, and we have pursued God together. I don't think friendships in the kingdom of God remain unless they are started and birthed in God's manifest presence.

Rob: True! Crying out together and pursuing His presence is definitely a great way to sustain those friendships. I don't know if you are a *Lord of the Rings* fan, but you might remember the "fellowship of the ring." This fellowship was close and intimate because of what they experienced together. So the same thing is true with people who experience the presence of God together. We could call these people "the fellowship of the kingdom." I want to move to another aspect of sustaining a kingdom culture. This last spring I was in Oklahoma doing a meeting, and you called me and talked about a biblical template.

Dan: Oh yes, the Lord gave me this vision of how we could sustain a kingdom culture or a fivefold apostolic culture in a church. I believe it would perpetuate transformation of a city, too, not just a church. The Lord gave me "eight Ps" that I believe are essential pillars to sustaining and perpetuating a move of God.

Rob: Let's walk through them. By the way, these pillars are not just for the Church. Individual believers need to function in these as well.

Dan: You go ahead and list them off. You know what they are.

Rob: Alright, the first pillar is *prayer*. There is no way we can sustain a move of God without constant prayer. And I'm not talking about being a church with a prayer ministry but rather becoming houses of prayer. Jesus said, "And He said to them, 'It is written, My HOUSE SHALL BE CALLED A HOUSE OF PRAYER'" (Matthew 21:13). That was the first pillar in this vision you had, right?

Dan: Oh yeah! We must be a house of prayer. In reality, the house of God shouldn't be anything else but a place that seeks after His presence. The word for prayer Jesus used in Matthew 21:13 comes from the root word that means to worship. So a church has to be a house of prayer. Prayer is the main thing because prayer is about worshipping Him. It's about seeking His presence all the time.

Rob: Churches need to figure out when this should happen corporately, too. It could be Sunday nights, Tuesday mornings, or Wednesday nights. It doesn't matter when it happens, but it should be more than merely talking about prayer. Believers need to cry out together. It doesn't have to look like any other service or any other ministry, but it certainly has to be a place where people corporately petition God together.

Dan: You know, when the early church was threatened, they corporately prayed together (see Acts 4:24). I believe churches are being threatened today. I think we're under attack. We need to cry out together. The Church needs to lift her voice before God and pray.

Rob: Paul said, "With all prayer and petition, pray at all times in the Spirit" (Ephesians 6:18a). Pray with every kind of prayer and do it at all times. We need to do that. The second pillar is *praise*.

Dan: I think that if we pray together, then we will worship together. I believe God inhabits our praise. I believe God loves worship, and He dwells where there are people who are focused on Him. Think about this: we become what we see. Praise and worship is focusing our attention on Jesus, and if we'll live to worship Him, then we'll become like Him. Worship is peeling back distractions and peeling back layers that have a way of creeping into our lives, keeping us from seeing Jesus. Constant praise keeps our perspective and view of God clean. If we are constantly praying, it will lead to praise.

These two pillars are vital if we are going to be a church that transforms a city. Praise is not about a style of worship music, either. True praise and worship is Spirit–led. It's done with total focus on Jesus. Worship is not about us. It is all about Jesus. It is all about our King. It is all about our Father. Regardless of what styles of music we use to worship, we need to totally focus on Jesus.

Rob: You mentioned this. It is not the style nor is it the instruments or band. We were in a service recently where they sang acapella, and it was beautiful. The presence of God just filled the place, but it was Spirit–led worship. Dan, we have to stop treating worship like cereal filler until we get to the next thing. Praise needs to be Spirit–led and Spirit–directed. We shouldn't just fill a time slot in a service. David said that he waited and waited for the Lord. He waited patiently for Him. And finally the Lord put a new song in his mouth (see Psalm 40:1–3). We need to wait in praise and worship long enough until the Spirit starts to sing through us.

Dan: That's good.

Rob: The third pillar is *presence*.

Dan: This pillar is so important, maybe the most important one, because if we don't have His presence everything is a man–made function. This might be the reason that we feel compelled to have an order of worship or service formats—we feel like we need to "do something" in case God doesn't show up. Yet when His presence rests upon us there is a shift in the atmosphere, and there is an opening into the possibilities of God. An extravagance of love, hope, and expectancy are poured out upon people when His presence fills a sanctuary. When we pray God answers, and when we worship He dwells with us. When He comes and His presence fills the atmosphere, we become presence driven.

Our churches are either presence led or flesh led. Our programs are either directed by God or manipulated by man. When we're led by the presence of God, it is like following the cloud through our journey of life—the cloud by day and the fire by night. I believe that presence-driven churches will have lasting effects because the presence of God will not be able to be contained inside the walls of a church. The manifest presence of God will spill outside the walls of the church and touch a community. His presence will rest on all of God's people, and they will go forth and touch others with His presence.

Rob: We literally carry His presence. We host His presence. I love that thought, Dan, because we have the ability to shift the atmosphere of a place when we enter the room by what we carry on us— by *whom* we carry. Let's move on to the fourth pillar which is *prophecy*.

Dan: I believe that when the presence of God comes, Spirit-filled people will speak His words. The presence of God anoints our message. Our message comes out as God's Word—not what he said 2000 years ago but what He is saying right now. Prophecy is speaking what God is saying at the moment.

Rob: There you go!

Dan: I believe when the prophetic is released, healing, deliverance, words of knowledge, comfort, exhortation, edification, and faith are released through the anointed Word of God that's being spoken. Life in the kingdom is not in meat or drink, but it *is* in the Holy Spirit. A kingdom culture is a prophetic culture where the Spirit manifests with a timely Word. Jesus said that when He speaks, His Word is Spirit (see John 6:63). His Word and the Holy Spirit work together in a prophetic culture. I believe when the presence of God comes, everybody in that atmosphere can speak His words.

The Bible says in Acts 2:17-18, "And it shall be in the last days, God says, 'That I will pour forth of My Spirit on all mankind; and your sons and your daughters shall prophesy. . . .'" The true evidence of being Spirit–filled would be that all the sons and daughters will prophesy; they will begin speaking the words of God over God's people. Prophecy is vital to the community of faith, Rob. It's so important that Paul told us to especially choose that particular manifestation above the others (see 1 Corinthians 14:1).

Rob: You've already defined it, but what is prophecy?

Dan: The word means to speak or utter in the influence of the Spirit. It means to say what I hear

God saying to me. Listen, all of God's sheep hear His voice (see John 10:27). So if we hear what He's saying, we ought to be able to speak what He's saying. So we pray, and then we praise, which brings the presence, and out of the presence we are enabled to prophesy.

Rob: We desperately need prophetic cultures, Dan, where men and women are hearing and releasing His words. The fifth pillar is *purity*.

Dan: When God's Word goes forth, truth is released because His Word is truth according to Jesus, and we are sanctified by the truth (see John 17:17). When the Word showed up in the temple, He had to cleanse the temple because he wanted a pure temple (see Matthew 21:12). The Bible says, "Your body is a temple of the Holy Spirit" (1 Corinthians 6:19). Unless we allow Him to purify us with the power of His Word, He won't be able to fill us completely to His satisfaction, and without the fullness of the Spirit, we can't change our world. So this pillar is purity. We can call it holiness, character of Christ, or sanctification, but it has to happen. Purity takes place when the Word of God is released out of the anointing.

Rob: The sixth pillar is *power*.

Dan: That is the other wing we talked about earlier. When a person becomes pure, they are not afraid to release the power of the Spirit in miracles, signs, wonders, deliverances, healings, transformations, reconciliations, restorations, and the breaking of bondages and addictions. All of these blessings are only possible in the power of God's Spirit, but they will not happen consistently until the Church becomes holy and pure—a spotless bride. When the temple is cleansed, miracles will take place, and everybody will run to the church and say, "Why haven't we heard about this before now?" People will be drawn to God. Miracles and power will happen when we become pure. It's just that simple.

Rob: That's what happened after Jesus cleansed the temple in Mathew 21:14. He purified the temple of those who were buying and selling, and He overturned the tables of the money changers. After He cleansed the temple, it says the blind and lame came to Him, and He healed them. So power followed purity. Let's move on, the seventh pillar is *partnership*.

Dan: I use the word partnership, but it's really discipleship. I believe that we have to give away what we have. Partnership is multiplication. We don't receive the Spirit of God to become a pool. We receive the Spirit to become a river. He doesn't give us life to hold on to it until we die. He gives us life so that we will die, and it will spring forth and touch many lives. So God wants to multiply what He puts into us. He put His seed into us—His Word inside of each of us—so that it will grow and multiply in the lives of people around the world. So I believe that partnership is discipleship making, which fulfills the commandment to make disciples. Discipleship is partnering with others until everyone is "partnered" into the family of God.

Rob: Our friend Craig Rench lives this pillar doesn't he?

Dan: Oh yes.

Rob: He wrote a book that will be listed in the Recommended Reading section entitled *The Master's Plan*. This book will help churches and leaders with the pillar of partnership. The eighth and final pillar is *perseverance*.

Dan: Persevering means that we keep doing all of these things until Jesus returns. We have to keep praying, keep praising, keep operating in the presence, keep operating in the prophetic, keep operating in purity, keep operating in power, keep bringing in partners, and keep persevering against all odds. If we don't persevere, we won't pass our faith on to the next generation. It is only in persevering that the true signs of apostles are manifested (see 2 Corinthians 12:12). Perseverance is so essential to an apostolic culture.

Perseverance is what the first-century church was known for, and it is what this last day's church will be known for — those who will persevere . . . those who will never quit or shrink back. We simply keep doing what we're supposed to do until the end. It is like the first Beatitude. We stay poor in spirit until we are persecuted, which forces us back to being poor in spirit. It is an unending cycle of going deeper into the heart of God and living the life of Jesus. We never stop!

Rob: These pillars are excellent, and we're implementing them in our church. The one that challenges me the most is this last one. Many people easily start races but few finish them. I want to finish in Christ, Dan. I want to pass my baton on to the next generation. The writer of Hebrews told us to, "Run with endurance the race that is set before us" (Hebrews 12:1). We must persevere! I'm praying that each person reading this book will feel encouraged to stay in the race.

Don't quit! Keep sowing into the Spirit because you *will* reap a harvest if you don't lose heart and give up (see Galatians 6:8–9).

Dan: Amen.

Rob: This template is not an "overnight program" to success. It should be integrated into our lives. It needs to become a lifestyle for all of us, and if we will live these pillars, then I believe that we will sustain a kingdom culture.

Dan: I agree, Rob.

I want to list the eight pillars Dan discussed as value statements that our church has embraced. Additionally, I look at them as personal commitments I am attempting to live. These pillars will not be evident in our church if they aren't evident in my life.

1. Prayer: We believe prayer moves mountains, demolishes strongholds, and reaches the nations; therefore, we desire to be a house of prayer.
2. Praise: We believe worship is an earthly exercise of an eternal experience; therefore, we live to glorify God.
3. Presence: We believe everything we do should be centered on Jesus and His manifest presence.

4. Prophecy: We believe the testimony of Jesus is a spirit of prophecy; therefore, in His presence we can hear and speak His voice.

5. Purity: We believe the work of the cross produces holiness in our hearts and lives; therefore, any and all sin can be cleansed.

6. Power: We believe our lives can be empowered by the extraordinary, outrageous, supernatural functions of the Holy Spirit.

7. Partnership: We believe Christians exist in community; therefore, outreach and discipleship are central to the gospel and the sustainability of the Church.

8. Perseverance: We believe Christians must steward and sustain a revival culture; therefore, we must prevail through challenges with an increasing hunger for God.

It is not our intent to create a paradigm for every church to emulate. While we believe that these eight pillars are biblical and essential to sustaining a kingdom culture, you may have found others that are more vital for your setting. By all means listen to the voice of the Holy Spirit. Pray, fast, and seek the counsel of God, but whatever you decide, please sustain a kingdom culture in your life and ministry.

I want to underscore perseverance. I mentioned during the interview that perseverance is the pillar that challenges me the most. Regardless of what list of values or pillars you decide on, this much is for sure: you will have to persevere in your life and ministry if you ever hope to accomplish something significant for the kingdom of God. I believe perseverance is most challenging because in our American culture we detest waiting. We have everything from express mail to microwave ovens and fast food to overnight shipping. We are impetuous people who desire instant results, and we don't like having to endure trials, hardships, and difficulties. Yet, everything I read in the Scripture indicates that those who finished well were those who endured the most, and they persevered until they experienced the breakthrough that they believed was possible.

Paul entered the city of Ephesus for the first time and found twelve guys who had been baptized under John's ministry. After explaining Jesus Christ to them, they were baptized in His name and received the Holy Spirit. Being forced out of teaching in the synagogue by hardened and disobedient people, Paul began reasoning *daily* in the school of Tyrannus and he did the same regiment for two years. He never stopped teaching the Word! He never quit or shrank back.

One scholar indicated that Paul taught the Word for more than 3,000 hours over a period of two years. He kept sowing into the Spirit until breakthrough was experienced. A mighty revival broke out in the city of Ephesus, and people began confessing their sins and turned to Christ. They burned their cultic books and ceased practicing magic. The Bible says, "So the word of the Lord was growing mightily and prevailing" (Acts 19:20). The Word of God became so widely known that everyone who lived in Asia heard it (see Acts 19:10). That is a remarkable report to say the least, but it occurred because one man refused to quit. Paul persevered until the kingdom of God came to Ephesus and made a transformational difference.

What about your city? I've pastored in Columbus, Ohio, since 1997, and we still have so much work to do. Our city hasn't experienced a major breakthrough yet, but we continue sowing the Word. We're making inroads into the community one life at a time. We're praying for people to be born again, we're crying out for bodies to be healed, we're seeking God for marriages and families, and we're pressing into His presence believing for a mighty outpouring of God's Holy Spirit on our church and every church in our city. We must persevere through trials and adversities. We have to believe Isaiah when he declared that we will pass through the waters and fire without being harmed (see Isaiah 43:2). Victory is always found on the other side of the greatest challenges if we'll simply persevere and never quit.

Dan mentioned that the early church in the book of Acts was known for its perseverance. That's true. Read the accounts of this persevering church. They didn't cease proclaiming the Word no matter what happened to them. When threatened because of their boldness, they cried out for even *more* boldness. When told to be silent about the faith, they refused to listen to any other voice except God's voice. When they were persecuted and flogged for their faith, they celebrated God that they were worthy enough to suffer for Him. And in the end most of them were martyred for choosing Jesus over the world because they knew it was the only way to bring Him *to* the world.

What's our excuse? What's our reason for quitting? What prevents us from persevering? Is it because people are leaving our churches? Is it because the pastor preaches too long? Is it because the music is too loud? Is it because we got fired from our job? Is it because our prayer hasn't been answered yet? What keeps us from persevering until the breakthrough is realized in our lives? The early believers were unceasing and relentless in their pursuit of God and in their mission to bring the kingdom to the entire world. They persevered and because they did, the Church of Jesus Christ prevailed.

My challenge to you is to determine this minute that you will not shrink back (see Hebrews 10:38). We must pass our legacy of faith onto the next generation, but we dare not lose any ground in the process. Keep pressing into the manifest presence of Jesus—even if there are sleepy-eyed, lazy people all around you. Keep believing God for signs, miracles, and wonders—even if you are criticized and called a proponent of "strange fire." Keep praying for healing even though people are sick and diseased because the Word still says the prayer of faith will save the sick (see James 5:15). Believe God for the revival, trust Him for those marriages, and remain faithful to your calling no matter what. Persevere to the end, my friends, because breakthrough is just around the corner.

Chapter Nine

THE MINISTRY OF HEALING

I believe that Jesus intended the ministry of healing to continue in our day and nothing in the New Testament would convince me otherwise. When Jesus commissioned His disciples to go into the world, He desired that our message would encompass spiritual, emotional, and physical healing. Any student of the book of Acts and the history of the Church during the first few centuries will observe that healing was normative in the life of God's people. However, over the course of time, events have occurred that have diminished the church's obligation to practice the ministry of healing. This chapter, which will probably be one of the longest chapters, is dedicated to helping revive that ministry.

Dan has witnessed the healing of thousands of people in his ministry, and so he's certainly qualified to talk about this subject. But let me encourage you that we are all qualified to heal as His disciples. I hope that you will combat any lie that says otherwise. We are all filled with the same Holy Spirit that Jesus was filled with, and we have all been commissioned to do what Jesus did (see John 14:12, 20:21). Nothing is impossible for God, and God has taken up residence within you through the Holy Spirit. His healing power is in you, and you simply need to take the risk and trust that God desires to use you.

Paul prayed that God is "able to do far more abundantly beyond all that we ask or think, according to the power that works within us" (Ephesians 3:20). Did you note what that verse is saying? The supernatural power of God is inside us! Let's not hold God in. Let's allow Him out to touch, heal, and restore people. He will accomplish far more than we could ever ask or think.

Rob: Dan, you have witnessed thousands of people healed for several years. This book is called, *Holiness and Healing*, so let's talk about healing.

Dan: I have one burning passion in my life, Rob, and it's to see God set the Church on fire. Then we won't be ashamed of the gospel. Paul said in Romans 1:16, that he wasn't ashamed of the gospel because it was power for salvation. The word "salvation" means to be forgiven, delivered, set free, and made whole. It is a powerful word. The best description I can find for that word salvation in the Bible is Isaiah 53:5 where Isaiah says that Jesus was wounded for our transgressions. That means that He forgives us for what we've "done." He was wounded for our wrong activities — the sins of our lives. Aren't you glad He does that?

This passage goes on to say that He was bruised for iniquities. That means He goes deeper than forgiveness, and He can change our very nature. He purges us from the essence of sin and changes our DNA. In 2 Peter it says that we partake of the divine nature. It is true that we become what we eat. That is why Jesus said, "Eat my flesh," in John 6. He wants us to become little *Christ*ians. If we partake of Him, then we become what He is.

This passage in Isaiah goes on to talk about chastisement and the peace of God that is given because of it. This is emotional well-being, and it is only possible through the chastening that Jesus endured. You will never be emotionally free unless you follow Jesus all the way to the cross and get to the other side. And finally, by His deep cuts and His stripes, this passage says we were totally healed. So this passage in Isaiah is a picture of salvation. It's a description of healing, forgiveness, deliverance, cleansing, and wholeness. I believe in it, Rob.

Rob: Give me some reasons for believing that God still heals today. There are a lot of people with a lot of opinions on the matter. So why do you believe in healing?

Dan: I have seven reasons for believing that God still heals today.

Rob: Let's walk through them.

Dan: First, I believe that it is God's will to heal. I hear people pray, "God, if it is your will, heal them." I hear that over and over again, but I've never heard anyone say, "God if it is your will, save them." I've already said that the word "save" encompasses a spiritual, physical, and emotional healing. But let me explain why I think it is God's will to heal.

In Genesis, God created the first man and woman with no sickness. He said mankind possessed His image and that it was good. So originally, there was no sickness so it must have been God's will. At the very end when we enter the new heaven, God will wipe away every tear and there will be no more sorrow, no more death, and no more effects of sin forever (see Revelation 21:4). Originally and eternally God's will was, and will be, for wholeness and healing.

It got messed up in the middle because of sin, but God didn't change His mind in the middle because He is a God who changes not. I also believe it is God's will because of how prevalent it was in the life and ministry of Jesus (see Hebrews 13:8). Jesus said in John 1:18, "No one has ever seen God at any time; the only begotten God who is in the bosom of the Father, He has explained Him." The word "explain" means to exegete (to explain, unfold, or expound something). Jesus is the exegesis of the Father's heart. Jesus is our pattern, our forerunner, our equipper, and the one who sticks closer than a brother. Jesus said He and the Father were one (see John 10:30).

In John 14:9, He says if you have seen me you have seen the Father. In Colossians 1:19, we're told that all of God's deity dwells in one body — namely, Jesus. In Hebrews 1:2–3, we're told that God speaks through Jesus and that Jesus is the exact representation of the Father. Jesus' ministry was more about healing and deliverance than it was about teaching and preaching. Therefore, if Jesus represents the Father, healing represents the Father.

Rob: Yes, and we're to represent Jesus.

Dan: Rob, when we remove the Christmas and Easter events in the gospels, there are about twenty-eight days of recorded history in the life and ministry of Jesus over three and a half years. There are forty-one miracles, which are more than one a day. There are more miracles than sermons. God must be more interested in healing the world than preaching to the world if Jesus is the exegesis of the Father's heart!

In Mark 1:40 a leper ran to Jesus and worshipped Him, and then he said, "If you are willing, will you cleanse me?" The Bible says that Jesus was "moved with compassion" (Mark 1:41). This phrase "moved with compassion" comes from a root word that actually means to be deeply agitated. Jesus hates what sin has done to His creation. He hates the effects of the fall. He is angered at it because we were made perfect. He went on to say "I am willing." The phrase "I am" is the present tense meaning that He was willing then, He is willing now, and He will be willing forever. He never changes. Jesus could be called the "willing God."

Rob: Yes, I agree, Dan. He was and is willing to heal.

Dan: Obviously, God doesn't always get His way on the earth, but we've been instructed to pray a powerful prayer. We're told to pray for His kingdom to come and His will to be done on earth as it is in heaven (see Matthew 6:10; Luke 11:2). We need more of an invasion down here of what is going on in heaven. In His realm there is no sickness. It wasn't affected by the fall. There is no depression, there is no pornography, there is no addiction, there is no cancer, there is no diabetes, and there are no heart issues in His kingdom. There is not a "bad section" in heaven. The kingdom is good everywhere. Jesus instructed us to pray each day for His kingdom to come. How do you know when the kingdom of God comes? We know when we see that His will is done here on earth as it is in heaven.

In 1 John 3:5, we learn that Jesus came to forgive us of our sins, and in 1 John 3:8, we learn that He came to destroy the devil's works. In Matthew 16 we learn that we're to unite and bind what has already been bound in heaven, and we're too loose what has already been loosed in heaven. It's like Jesus is saying, "I'm trying to get you caught up with what's already done in heaven." Things are running just fine in heaven . . . now it's time to pull that down here. It's time to destroy the works of the devil!

Now He doesn't always get His way, but it is not on His end. I'll explain it this way: there is this fight going on between God's kingdom and the fallen kingdom of this world. We know the prince and power of this era referred to in Isaiah 14 and Ezekiel 28, which is Satan, was kicked out of heaven with a third of the angels and has been wreaking havoc in this realm. But Jesus has dominion over both realms — this realm and the kingdom of God. It says in Matthew 12 that He has dominion over this age and the age to come, and it states the same in Ephesians 1:21. He has dominion over this fallen age and the age to come (Revelation 21:4).

So I'll explain to you the battle we are in and why we don't always see the breakthrough as Jesus did. Think of two circles coming together. One circle is an example of the kingdom of darkness. That was the time when Adam and Eve sinned and everything changed. Our world was filled with sin, sickness, and disease because of the fall of man — not because of God's will. Then the next circle represents the age to come or the kingdom of God. This is the realm of heaven where everything is whole, restored, and perfect. Now when Jesus came to earth, He brought His kingdom into the kingdom of darkness. So there is an overlap of these two realms. We are living in the middle of the overlap. Our present age could be called the "already not yet" age because we've experienced the kingdom of God but not to its complete fullness as when we're all in heaven [see illustration].

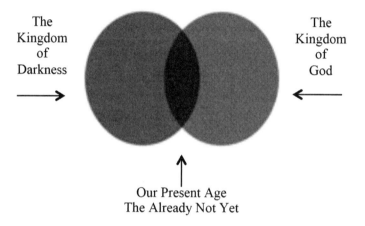

The
Kingdom
of
Darkness

⟶

The
Kingdom
of
God

⟵

↑
Our Present Age
The Already Not Yet

We are in this fallen age, but we are also in the age to come because Jesus said the kingdom is already in us (see Luke 17:21). So our responsibility is to manifest the kingdom of God in this present age. Jesus' ministry was an example of manifesting the kingdom of God in this present age. Every single time He would transform a lost person, a demoniac, a crippled person, someone who was broken, or someone who was destitute, He was bringing His kingdom to them. He manifested it because He fully operated out of the kingdom of God.

So here we are. Some people get saved, some people get sanctified, some people get healed, and some people don't. There is tension because we are in the "already not yet" moment. It's a battle between two realms. But we can't settle for what is, Rob. Are we supposed to live our whole lives merely studying the Word, serving people, and worshipping God but never manifesting the kingdom of God in this realm? I believe everything about our Christian life is about bringing heaven to earth. Am I right?

Rob: Absolutely, you are right. We've already said this, but we're to live exactly as Jesus did. If He manifested the kingdom of God in this present age, then our commission is the same.

Dan: Matthew 6:10 is my life's verse because I want my whole life to be given to one purpose, and that is to bring His realm into this realm. When the kingdom of God comes, everything changes. Jesus was 100 percent successful in His ministry because He didn't struggle between the two kingdoms. He only did what the kingdom of God did. He focused on one kingdom. And listen, the beauty of this is that now He lives in each of us.

My picture of Jesus is this: He is the narrow point of the hourglass of eternity, and all the resources of the King's domain, healing, holiness, direction, provision, correction, comfort, and love all flows into the spot where Jesus is [see illustration]. We take all of heaven's resources and dispense them into our realm. He is the narrow spot, the narrow way, and He lives inside us. However, all of heaven's resources are trapped in heaven if Jesus isn't allowed to function through us. We can impede or deter heaven's resources from touching earth if we're not functioning in obedience or faith.

The Heavenly Realm

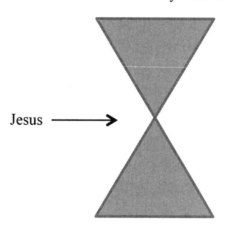

Jesus ⟶

The Earthly Realm

Rob: Well, that was reason number one as to why you believe healing is for today. What is the second reason?

Dan: My second reason for believing that healing is for today is because Jesus demonstrated it. We've already mentioned this, but let me go a bit deeper with this reason. Jesus is our pattern to follow (see John 13:15). In 1 John 2:6, we're told that if we claim to be a Christian, then we are going to walk as He walks. Jesus said in John 5:19 that apart from the Father He couldn't do anything. He was not just saying that to stretch the truth. He meant every word if it. He needed His Dad to do what He did. "I can only do what I see what my Father is doing," Jesus said. So the first key to unlocking the healing ministry the way Jesus did it was to stay so intimate with the Father that you are always aware of what He is up to.

Rob, you always talk about staying at the feet of Jesus. Corey Jones always talks about remaining poor, and Rhonda Hughey talks about being the Father's wrecking ball. I love all of these analogies because if we will stay intimate with the Father, then we will always be aware of what He's doing. If we're intimate with Him, then we will realize that He desires to do something all the time, but He is just waiting for someone who actually has their eyes completely on Him. God actually will do what He desires *through* us if we'll stay intimate with Him. Peter described

Jesus' ministry success this way: "God anointed Him with the Holy Spirit and with power, and how He went about doing good and healing all who were oppressed by the devil, for God was with Him" (Acts 10:38).

If 40 percent of the gospels are about the miracles of Jesus then I think that they are important, and we should be wondering how, why, and what happened to us if we're not duplicating what Jesus did. The question is: are we really Christlike disciples? I believe that we should study all of the gospels—not just part of them. We should study the whole life of Jesus. In John 14:12, Jesus said that if anyone believed in Him, and that is present tense faith (meaning that if we are *believing* Him), then they would do what He did. So if we are intimate enough with Jesus and leaning into Him with faith, then we will do what He did and even greater. That means "anyone" who believes on Him.

So there is no ministry except the ongoing ministry of Jesus. There is not a Nazarene, Pentecostal, Catholic, or Lutheran ministry. The only ministry that is real ministry is the ongoing ministry of Jesus. Anyone who leans on Him will start to do *His* ministry and even greater things. Matthew 28:18 tells us that Jesus extended His authority to each of us, so we are to go and make disciples of every nation. We're to baptize in the name of the Father, Son, and Spirit. We're to teach others to do what Jesus did. And doing what He did will be inclusive of healing and miracles.

Rob: That's an interesting way to put it: we only have Jesus' ministry. I hear people talk about their ministry, but in reality we only have one ministry.

Dan: The only ministry that we have, Rob, is the ongoing ministry of doing what Jesus did. What did Jesus do? He did whatever needed to be accomplished at the moment, and He did it as the Father instructed Him. He would extend forgiveness. He healed the sick, He cast out demons, and He even raised the dead. Peter said that Jesus was a man attested in front of people with signs, wonders, and miracles that the Father did through Him (see Acts 2:22).

Rob: And we can't dismiss doing the things that Jesus did by stating that He was God because He gave up His "omni" (unlimited power) abilities. He functioned as a man filled with God.

Dan: He did. We learn in Philippians 2 that Jesus emptied himself of the right to be God, and He came to earth born of a woman, raised in a carpenter's shop, called into ministry, and baptized by a guy with locust breath. He came up out of the water, and His whole life was dependent on the Holy Spirit's empowerment. Jesus was God, but He gave up His right to divinity to show that it is possible for a man to be Spirit-filled, Spirit-empowered, Spirit-led, and Spirit-driven. If He wasn't functioning as a man, then why would Satan tempt him? God cannot be tempted (see James 1:13).

Here's another thought: His disciples asked at what time will the consummation of all things transpire, and Jesus responded that He didn't know. He said, "Only the Father knows." When Jesus prayed in Luke 22 and His disciples were sleeping, He went to them in anguish sweating drops of blood, and the angel came and strengthened Him. God doesn't need to be strengthened, but Jesus did and Jesus was our prototype. He demonstrated for us how to live and what it looks like for the original Nazarene to pull off revealing the Father's heart through the power of the Holy Spirit.

It's interesting to note that Jesus never did any miracles before He was baptized in the Spirit—at least they weren't recorded. As far as we know, Jesus didn't pull off any healing until He was baptized in the Spirit. He is our pattern, Rob. Jesus said that the Spirit of the Lord is upon Him. He said that He was anointed by the Lord. That is good news for the Church because if we are desperate and hungry, the anointed Word of the Holy Spirit of God is looking for you. If we aren't needy for His presence, then He can't use us, but if we come before Him poor and desperate, then the Spirit of the Lord will rest upon us and use us.

He will use us to set captives free and open the eyes of the blind just as the Father used Jesus. He will use us to proclaim liberty for the oppressed and to declare His day of salvation. When we are filled with the Spirit as Jesus was, we become the living epistle of God (see 2 Corinthians 2:2–3) and the fulfillment of the Scripture (see Luke 4:21).

Jesus then sends us into the world as He did His disciples, and we are clothed with His power. As living epistles, His Word is on our hearts, and His Spirit empowers us to heal the sick, cleanse the lepers, cast out demons, and raise the dead (see Matthew 10:8). Jesus had power to do these things through the Holy Spirit, and we have that same power. We will receive power when we're baptized in the Spirit (see Acts 1:8). The same power that He operated in is the same power that we operate in. Jesus was the original disciple maker, and we are to follow His pattern.

Rob: Amen. You know, functioning in the power of the Holy Spirit is the essence of the new covenant, isn't it?

Dan: It is, Rob. If you ask people in the Church why Jesus came to earth, most would tell you this: "He came to die on a cross to forgive us of our sins and to save us in order that we could go to heaven." That is a good answer, but the writers of the gospels never announced Jesus like that. Think about this: when someone is introduced, they are usually associated with something they do or will accomplish. In Matthew 3, Mark 1, Luke 3, and John 1, Jesus is introduced this way: "He came in order to baptize us with the Holy Spirit and fire."

The essence of the new covenant was to fill us with His Spirit. Why? The answer is He knows that we can't be little *Christians*, running around the world doing what He did unless we have the same Spirit within us that He operated with. That is how Jesus did what He did — through the power of the Spirit. So the new covenant was not Jesus dying on the cross; rather, Jesus dying on the cross appropriated a new and better covenant (see Hebrews 8:6), which is the Spirit living inside us so that we can be just like Him.

Rob: What is the third reason that you believe in healing?

Dan: The third reason that I believe in healing is because of the kingdom of God. Once again, we're told to pray that His kingdom will come to earth as it is in heaven (see Matthew 6:10). That is just so simple, but when His kingdom comes into our world, His will starts to happen. So we are supposed to pray for the kingdom to invade this world. In Matthew 6:33 we're told to seek His kingdom before anything else. The pursuit of our life should be His domain. We are supposed to seek the kingdom of God.

In Matthew 10, Jesus commissioned us to preach, teach, and do ministry. He was saying: I'm going to give you all the authority that I have because I can't do this by myself. I can't cover the entire world without helpers. So come to Me, and I'll give you the authority. This is how you do it. When you preach, tell people that the kingdom is at hand. Then heal the sick, raise the dead, cast out demons, and cleanse lepers.

So we are supposed to preach the kingdom by demonstrating it. We are to live the kingdom. The kingdom doesn't come by your observation but by your demonstration. The kingdom is in us (see Luke 17:21). So live it! It's all about the kingdom and demonstrating kingdom activities. Jesus told us that the kingdom of God is at hand (see Matthew 4:17). So we need to repent, which literally means to change our thinking. We need to start thinking and acting as if the kingdom is near.

What happens when the kingdom is near? The will of God happens on earth as it is in heaven. Sin, disease, and sickness start to suffocate when the atmosphere of the kingdom is manifested in our realm. There is no sin in heaven so when the kingdom comes—when His domain comes, the kingdom of darkness bows to the kingdom of light. Light is always superior to darkness. If we turned off all the lights in this building and it was pitch black, there wouldn't be a battle for the light to penetrate the darkness when a switch is turned on. Light always wins!

So when the kingdom comes, whatever is happening in the King's domain in heaven starts happening here. So if there is no sickness there, then healings happen here. If there is no sin there, then forgiveness starts happening here. If there is no carnality there, then purity starts happening here. Revelation 21:27 tells us that nothing is impure or unclean up there, so we should expect no carnal natures here because if the kingdom comes, then people's hearts will be purified.

Rob: When the kingdom of God comes, Dan, it exposes deeds done in darkness. It reveals whatever isn't like the kingdom of light.

Dan: It's interesting to note that in the Old Testament there is very little talk about demons. There are a few places like the prince of Persia with Daniel's delay and Ezekiel seeing Satan fall. There are a couple of places in the Old Testament where leviathan is mentioned and a couple of demonic spirits identified like a lying spirit, a spirit of Egypt, and a spirit of harlotry. We are talking about 4,000 years of history with only a handful of notations of the demonic realm. But in the New Testament when the kingdom of God comes, demons flare up everywhere. Why? Because when the kingdom of heaven comes, the dark kingdom is no longer able to hide.

In Matthew 8 the demons recognized Jesus. They looked at Jesus who was full of the kingdom and said something like, "If you are going to pull the trigger, at least put us in some pigs." The demons thought that they were going to be tormented before their time. In other words when Jesus brought the kingdom of God, it took the demonic realm off guard. Paul said we are not unaware of the Devil's schemes (see 2 Corinthians 2:11). They should actually be unaware of our schemes. If we are bringing the kingdom of God with us, then we should be freaking out the demonic realm. So when the kingdom comes, what is going on there begins happening here. So, I believe in healing because there is healing in the kingdom.

Rob: I do, too. What is your fourth reason?

Dan: The fourth reason that I believe in healing is because of the authority of God. Think for a moment about the commissioning accounts. By the way, it is never "missional." We've been given a "co-mission" because it was always meant to be accomplished *with* God. It's not go, do the best we can, and He will back us. It is more like let's go have fun together because He is living inside of us. So we're co-missioned with Him to do His will.

Anyway, in Mark 3 Jesus called His disciples to come be with Him. I love that because before He gives us all authority to do His works and greater things, He would like for us to know Him. He wants us to be with Him so that we will represent Him exactly. So He first called them to be with Him, and then He gave them "authority" to cast out demons and preach the kingdom. In Luke 5 Jesus was in a crowded room, and four guys cut a hole in the roof to let a guy down. In this passage it says that the power of God was available to heal. There is a difference between power and authority. Power is the ability, but authority is the right or the privilege to use the ability.

Jesus saw this guy on the mat, and He saw their faith. The first thing that He did was to forgive this guy's sins. I love that because it demonstrates that Jesus will always minister to us in the area of our greatest need. If we need forgiveness, then that is what we will receive. If we need healing, then that is what we will receive. Not one time did Jesus fail to heal someone who came to Him in need of a healing. Jesus healed people every time they needed it.

So He forgives the guy because that is the beginning of salvation—to be forgiven, cleansed, and made whole. Then Jesus perceived what they were thinking because He operated in the gifts of the Spirit. Remember that He is actually the original Nazarene, and we are to be just like Him.

He discerned what they were thinking, and He asked which would be easier, to forgive sins or to heal the lame man so that he could walk. Then Jesus healed the guy on the mat to demonstrate that He not only had the power, but also He had the authority to heal.

Rob: And we have been given the authority as well as power, too.

Dan: Yes, it's true. Jesus' authority wrecks me because I don't completely understand it. The centurion came to Jesus and said that his servant was sick. Jesus offered to go to his house, but the centurion refused because he was not worthy. The centurion told Jesus to merely "say the word," for he knew that his servant would be healed through the authority of Jesus' Word. Then the centurion said, "For I also am a man under authority . . ." (Matthew 8:9a). Did you note the word "also" in this verse? The centurion recognized the authority that Jesus was operating under.

Isn't it amazing that outsiders recognized the authority on Jesus but the Pharisees missed it? Isn't it amazing that someone can be devoted to the Scripture, devoted to a movement, devoted to an institution, and devoted to a denomination, and sometimes entirely miss the authority that Christ has and the authority that He's given to us?

Jesus healed the centurion's servant because He operated under authority. In Luke 9 Jesus called his disciples unto Himself, and He gave them power and authority to heal the sick, to cast out demons, and to preach the kingdom. In Luke 10 He sent seventy-two others out. He gave them power and authority to step on the enemy by healing the sick and preaching the nearness of the kingdom. In reality, that must have been a boring sermon. Heal the sick and then preach this message, "The kingdom is near." How many points? Well, "The-kingdom-is-near," I guess four points!

Rob: That's so funny.

Dan: It's true, Rob. But think for a moment, how did the disciples pull off their miracles?

Rob: They operated under His authority.

Dan: Think about this: Jesus never prayed for a person to be made well, He never prayed for a person to be forgiven, and He never prayed to heal someone. He just spoke with authority and commanded demons to flee and sickness to leave. He was under the Father's authority so Jesus was able to speak to whatever was in His way. His prayer life was astonishing when it comes to a healing ministry because there was none — at least at the moment.

Rob: Exactly! He prayed and fasted, but it wasn't at the moment of crisis. In other words, Jesus prayed and fasted into a lifestyle. Because He prayed in private, He was equipped to function with power and authority in public. For example, Jesus healed a demon-possessed boy and told His disciples that it can only happen through prayer (see Mark 9:29). Yet, Jesus didn't pray for the boy to be healed at that moment. His life was already filled with prayer and fasting, so His spiritual reservoir was deep enough to make decrees of healing.

Dan: This is why Jesus would say: "Take your bed home" or "straighten up, rise up, stretch forth your hand." I mean, He never prayed for healing. He just used authority and spoke to the situation. He is the pattern for us to follow because He is the original Nazarene, and someday I want to get to that level. Don't you?

Rob: Yes, I want to, Dan. I want to be just like Jesus.

Dan: There are three times in the gospels where we are told that a student is never above His teacher, but when we are fully trained, we will be exactly like Him. Jesus said that! I don't believe that there is ever one person saved, healed, or delivered because of how good we are praying. It is only because we are praying in the authority that God has given to us. Jesus never commanded the disciples to pray for sick people. He simply told them to do it. I'm not there yet, but I want to be more like Jesus.

Rob: I'm not either, Dan. To be honest, sometimes I find myself praying over someone who needs healing merely to generate faith in my heart. I want to get the place where my faith is so immersed in Him that I can speak with authority over people in need. Why don't people operate with this divine authority that Jesus has given to us?

Dan: I believe that there are three reasons. First, people in the Church don't use the authority that they have because they are biblically illiterate. If we actually knew the Word of God, we would know the power that has been given to us. Jesus told some religious people that they were in error because they didn't know the Word of God (see Mathew 22:29). Jesus went on to say that if we don't know the Word, then we won't know the power of God. So we have to really know the Word so that we would actually know the authority that Jesus has given to us.

Second, people fail to function with authority because of disappointments. We might pray for someone and they will die, or we pray for cancer to be removed and it remains. We convince ourselves that it must not be our gift, and we talk ourselves out of the authority we carry. We come into an agreement with sickness or disease and suppose that God is using it for some reason, so we cease speaking with authority over the need. Jesus never blessed sickness. He never left someone struggling in a disease so that God could teach them a lesson.

I believe that disappointments have a way of eroding our expectations, which then erodes our faith, which then erodes our authority, and as a result, we start to make up new doctrines in the midst of our disappointments. Rob, I can't always explain why healing doesn't take place when we command it to leave, but Jesus spoke with authority over sick people and healed them. So if He did, then I can . . . I must do it—I have no other option.

Third, I don't think authority will ever work if we don't take the risk that God is telling us to take. If God tells you to go across the aisle at Walmart and pray for that lady who has three kids and who is overwhelmed, then we need to step out and do what He's telling us to do. We have no idea what God could do through us in our obedience. He desires to flow through us and touch people everywhere we go, but the authority of God will never work unless we are willing to take the risk. Does that make sense?

Rob: Totally! When I've stepped out in obedience, God has amazed me. If we're obedient with small things, I believe it sets us up for greater things, too.

Dan: Amen, Rob. The fifth reason that I believe in healing is because of faith. I don't fully understand faith, but I'm glad Jesus said that I only need a tiny mustard seed of faith and that it will be good enough. Our faith must be in Jesus and not in our own faith. We are told to look unto Jesus (see Hebrews 12:2). If our eyes are looking unto Jesus, then He will perfect our faith. Think about that: He is the one who perfects what He has already given to us if our eyes are on Him.

Faith often operates in various directions, too. For example, the woman in Luke 8 touched Jesus' prayer shawl. She possessed the faith. She pressed through the crowd and touched Him, so her faith apprehended a miracle. Jesus told the man in John 5, beside the pool of Bethsaida, to pick up his mat and walk, and when he did, the miracle came. In that story, Jesus initiated the faith. In Mark 2 the four guys tore a hole in the roof and lowered their friend down on a home-made elevator, and a miracle happened because of *their* faith. Faith works in every direction as long as it's fixed on Jesus. You don't have to have a lot of faith. You just have to believe in Him and believe that He will make a difference in your life. So I'm learning about faith.

Rob: I'm learning about faith, too, because without faith it's impossible to please God. Completely impossible (see Hebrews 11:6)!

Dan: I like the story in Mark 9 about faith. This guy brought his son to the disciples because he was possessed by demons. The demons threw his son into the water and he had epileptic seizures, but the disciples were unable to cast the demon out. So the father went to Jesus and said some-thing like, "Hey, I brought my boy to your disciples and nothing happened." This is how Jesus responded, "O unbelieving generation, how long shall I be with you? How long shall I put up with you . . ." (Mark 9:19)?

That's an interesting response. You can be a gang member, drug addict, prostitute, tax evader, murder, and an adulterer, and Jesus will not get upset with you when you come to Him in repentance. But if you are His disciple—a person who has been given all authority and you don't use it, Jesus gets really annoyed. Jesus was asking, "How long shall I tolerate your unbelief?" He didn't wait until He was in a small group to correct them. He was right in the middle of church! Jesus was not "seeker sensitive" at that moment.

Rob: Jesus rebuked their lack of faith. In other words, as His disciples we should always be in a spiritual condition that is able to help people.

Dan: Yes, Jesus didn't coddle His followers at that moment. Anyway, the guy came to Jesus and said something like, "If you can do anything, take pity on us and help us." This makes me have to ask: How many people have gone to Jesus after we failed to do what He commissioned us to do? I wonder if the Church has given Jesus a bad reputation. So, this guy is broken and He said something like, "If you can do anything, can you help my boy?" Jesus told him that all things were possible for the one who believed, and this father responded, "I do believe; help my unbelief" (Mark 9:24). In other words, this father desired to believe and he didn't want to remain in his unbelief.

I have learned that faith is not the absence of doubt, but it's the evidence of belief in the midst of doubt. In John 6:29, we learn that the works of the Father are to believe in Him. Belief in the Father will eventually choke out doubt if we'll keep on believing no matter what. Belief is to doubt as light is to darkness. Constant belief penetrates doubt. In John 1 it says that light came into the world and the darkness could not overpower it because light trumps darkness. Belief trumps doubt if we'll keep on believing. So faith is not the absence of doubt. Faith is the presence of belief in the midst of doubt.

So back to our story, the disciples came to Jesus privately and asked Him why they failed. I'm glad that we can always go to Jesus in private and deal with our failures! Jesus talked with them about prayer, but as we've already said, Jesus didn't pray at that moment for the father's boy to be healed. His bank account of faith was already full because He lived a lifestyle of prayer.

Power and authority are based on what has hap-pened in us before we get to the moment of crisis. Faith is built in private moments of prayer and fasting, so when the crisis is before us, we have the anointing to speak with faith over the situa-tion. Rob, we cannot do the ministry of Jesus off last week's sermon. We can't function in power off last year's revival. What we did in our quiet time a few weeks ago will not suffice for today. We have to walk in His presence moment by moment. We have to pray without ceasing. The only way that we can live in faith is by staying full of our "daily bread" which is the Word of God (see Matthew 6:11; Romans 10:17).

Rob: Walking in the Spirit and walking in faith is essentially the same thing, Dan, and we do this moment by moment each day. So what is the sixth reason that you believe in healing?

Dan: The sixth reason that I believe in healing is because of the atonement. In my studies of the gospels, I learned that Jesus did all His miracles of healing before the atonement. He never did one healing after the crucifixion. They were all done before the cross. Matthew chapters eight and twelve quote Isaiah's prophecy about Jesus. Think about this: over seven hundred years before Jesus arrived on the scene, Isaiah prophesied that

Jesus would cure sickness, heal sorrows, cleanse sins, purify natures, and transform emotions, and He was going to do all of that before the atonement. Jesus showed the world what the Father's heart looked like. He demonstrated to the world what it looked like when the kingdom of heaven comes to earth, and it's housed in a vessel of flesh. The kingdom isn't limited to the flesh that it's in. If we'll let it out, the kingdom will touch and heal people wherever we go.

Rob: So how is the atonement related to healing?

Dan: The Bible says in 1 Peter 2:24, "And He Himself bore our sins in His body on the cross, so that we might die to sin and live to righteousness; for by His wounds you were healed." In 2 Corinthians 5:21 it says, "He made Him who knew no sin to be sin on our behalf, so that we might become the righteousness of God in Him." Righteousness means to stand before God as if we have never sinned. God desires that we are righteous people. This is really a big deal to Him. It was His original plan in the beginning that we would represent Him on the earth.

But sin marred that plan, so it required Jesus to take our sin upon Him so that we could acquire His righteousness. He became the essence of sin so that we could become the essence of righteousness. Peter wrote "by His stripes we are healed." The next verse explains the true healing that took place during Jesus' atonement. "For you were continually straying like sheep, but now you have returned to the Shepherd and Guardian of your souls" (1 Peter 2:25).

Jesus became sin so that all of us could truly become the righteousness of God. The stripes that Jesus received healed us, but what were we healed from? The answer is we were healed from the propensity or desire of running away from God like straying sheep. He removed not just our sins, guilt, and shame, but He healed the nature inside of us that pulled us in a different direction from God. His atonement healed us in the deepest way. It healed our nature so that we could run to the Shepherd. He healed us to the point that our deepest longing is to be with Jesus.

Now since the essence of sin has been atoned for, it's possible for every human to be healed spiritually, emotionally, and physically because the root of all sickness and disease is atoned for by the blood of Jesus. Sickness and disease are the result of sin that entered our world, but if you remove all sin from our lives through the atoning power of Jesus, then there is no room for sickness to remain in our lives either. Jesus' atonement removed all sin from our hearts, so I believe that all the effects of sin can be removed from my body and mind as well.

Rob: That's so good, Dan. That is what we talked about in regard to the word "salvation." Throughout the New Testament that word carried the idea of total healing physically, emotionally, and spiritually. We've usually associated the term salvation with only the removal of our sins, but it's much more than that.

Dan: It is, Rob. I have one more reason why I believe in healing. My seventh reason is because I have never been to a place where I didn't see someone healed. I've been brainwashed into believing this because I've seen so much. I just keep seeing miracles everywhere I go. I have seen tumors shrink, cancer cleansed, paralyzed limbs move, people get out of wheelchairs, and deaf ears opened. I remember being in St. Louis, Missouri, and this guy in a wheelchair was brought to me. He was in his pajamas, and when I asked him why he was in the chair, he said, "I-I-I-I," all he did was stutter. I asked his mother what happened, and she told me that he was struck by lightning at the age of twenty-four. He was thirty years old at the time of this meeting.

His name was Willie. I said, "Willie, do you want to get up?" He grabbed my hand and started to walk. He hadn't walked in six years.

Listen, it doesn't matter the age either. I laid hands on a woman in Gardner, Kansas, who was ninety-two years old, and she got out of her wheelchair and walked for the first time in ten years. I don't believe in healing because it is a theory or something that I've studied, I believe in it because it happens almost every day of my life. I've even seen people raised from the dead, Rob. This stuff is real. When the kingdom comes, everything changes. We don't need better strategies, we just need to believe that Jesus wants to flow out of us and touch a world.

Rob: Amen. You are seeing an increase in these things, too.

Dan: I am seeing more and more each day, Rob. God wants to heal people. It's His will to heal. It's His nature to heal. God is willing. You know, Jesus prayed that the Father would sanctify His disciples by the truth (see John 17:17). The only way that His disciples could do His ministry is they had to be sanctified by the truth. So here's my question: if we have experienced the truth and have been sanctified, but we didn't get our breakthrough when we prayed and therefore became offended and stopped believing the truth, are we still sanctified? The reason that I ask that is because Jesus says we are sanctified by the truth, and if we have compromised the truth because of hurt, disappointments, or offenses, then we are no longer in truth. Therefore, we are no longer walking in sanctification.

I believe that we have to stay in the truth to remain sanctified. His truth trumps everything else, too. His truth trumps our experiences and our circumstances. His truth is greater than our lack of breakthroughs. We have to keep believing His truth because His truth never changes. So, if we were really in the truth, then we would be doing what God sent Jesus to do—and even greater things still. That's the sanctified life, Rob, remaining in the truth and doing what He did (see John 14:12).

Rob: So you're saying that we can backslide out of our sanctification if we don't remain in the truth?

Dan: We can, Rob, I really believe that. If we don't believe His truth, then what are we trusting in?

Rob: Yes, good question.

Dan: The final thing that I want to say about healing is that all physical healing is temporary. The only healing that is eternal is spiritual healing. So even though God desires to heal our bodies, we will still die. Lazarus was raised from the dead, but he still died again. I hope everyone reading this will believe for healing no matter what, but I *really* hope that people will get their spiritual hearts healed. I want people to remain in the truth and stay sanctified. That's eternal healing.

Rob: Amen. Well said.

I believe in a healing ministry because I believe that it is biblical. I believe that we have been commissioned to heal the sick just as Jesus did. I believe that we have the same power in us that Jesus possessed. We don't have a lesser form of the Holy Spirit in us. Moreover, I have witnessed many miracles and healings in my church as well as in my travels. That being said, there is a mystery to this subject matter.

I'm amazed when someone is healed in a prayer line while someone standing next to them is not healed. I'm amazed when someone is healed instantaneously and others are healed over time. I'm also amazed when a sudden miracle of healing occurs in someone after years of praying. So I want to conclude this chapter with a few summary thoughts about keeping our faith in God's Word and not our circumstances. As Dan said, I don't want to get out of truth and put my faith in something else. Only His Word is truth (see John 17:17). Some things might be true, but His Word is truth; therefore, His Word should trump any situation that I'm in even if it's true. A doctor's report is true, but that doesn't make it truth.

No power is greater than His Word. Isaiah said that when God's Word is dispatched from His mouth, it will not return to Him empty (see Isaiah 55:11). That literally means that His Word will always carry an effect. It will never be dispatched in vain. There is tremendous power in His Word. Think about creation for a moment. The Spirit of God hovered over the surface of the waters, waiting with anticipation of one thing: the Word! The moment that God spoke chaos became order. Ezekiel encountered the same thing in a valley (see Ezekiel 37:1–10). He looked and saw nothing but a dry heap of bones, and these bones were very dry indeed. This valley was a chaotic mess. Can these bones live again, God asked? Then Ezekiel prophesied over this dusty mess. He spoke God's Word over the situation, and an army arose out of the dry heap. Just imagine what could happen when God's Word is released over your circumstances.

In the New Testament it was an out-of-covenant Roman centurion who recognized the power of the Word. He came to Jesus because his servant was paralyzed and tormented (see Matthew 8:6–8). Jesus offered to go and heal his servant, but the centurion refused because he didn't feel worthy of hosting Jesus in his home. Then he said these unforgettable words to Jesus, "Just say the word, and my servant will be healed" (Matthew 8:8). In other words, he realized that Jesus didn't need to be on the premises to heal someone. This centurion understood that Jesus' Word carried such amazing authority that once it is released it would fulfill its intended purpose. He had faith in the Word of the Lord. He trusted the Word over the circumstances that his servant was in. Jesus had never encountered faith like that—not even from His own disciples. Do you *really* believe the Word of the Lord?

What often happens to us is that our circumstances appear greater than the reality of His Word, and this opens to door to unbelief. The moment we elevate our present reality over God's Word is the moment we start to formulate doctrines that fit the context of our experiences. So let me ask you again: do you trust His Word when circumstances are contradictory to what His Word declares? There are people that I'm declaring healing over, but their circumstances have yet to change. Will I continue to declare God's Word over them or believe that my present reality trumps what He says?

The Word makes strong declarations about healing. For example: "The prayer offered in faith will restore the one who is sick" (James 5:15); "Heal the sick" (Matthew 10:8); and Jesus declared, ". . . The works that I do, he will do also . . ." (John 14:12). So whose report will I believe? I don't have the authority to change God's Word. My only obligation is to trust what He says. There are many other circumstances that are dry, chaotic, or even seem dead, but I'm speaking His Word over them. There are people bound by addictions, people steeped in sin, people overwhelmed by oppressions, and people broken and far from God. I cannot and I must not cease speaking God's Word over these situations because I believe His Word will prevail. I trust His Word even when I don't understand the circumstances because I believe there is power in what He says.

I've had people explain to me that they've gone to the altar during an invitation seeking to be healed, and nothing happened to them. So they reduced God's Word on the subject of healing and redefined it to match their limited situation. Bob Sorge said belief in God's Word to heal gives him the incentive and momentum to continue pursuing God. Sorge has been waiting and trusting God for his own healing but refuses to quit pursuing God on the matter because of what the Bible says. My friend Craig Rench told me about a woman who went forward to be healed fifty times and nothing happened to her, but on the fifty-first time she was instantly healed. What would have happened if she placed greater faith in her circumstances than in the Word of God? My guess is she would have quit pressing into God after about three or four times, and she probably wouldn't have been healed. We must always trust God's Word over our circumstances no matter how long we have labored.

So here's the question: what if physical healing never occurs this side of eternity? What if our circumstances never change? I have two responses for those questions. First, I hope that I will always stay in the truth regardless of my circumstances. Again, His Word is truth, and I cannot get out of truth no matter what. I agree with what someone once said to me, "I would rather die in faith than live with doubt." Cindy and I have walked through the valley of the shadow of death. We have seen and experienced the perils of cancer firsthand, and our healing didn't occur the way we had hoped or declared.

But this much is for sure: we didn't lose hope in the Word of God. To this day we have a stronger appreciation and appetite for the Word of God, and by God's grace we will always remain in His truth. We will put more faith in His Word than in our circumstances. It's just that simple for us.

Second, I absolutely agree with Dan about eternal healing. No matter how many healings I see or experience, the one that matters the most is spiritual healing. We must have our hearts healed from all sin. I can't explain all of the mysteries and nuances about healing, but I truly believe that one day I will live eternally with Jesus. I believe in an eternal heaven where there is no sorrow, mourning, or tears. There is an eternal dwelling that is totally void of all sin and sickness, and if our hearts have been cleansed and filled with Jesus, then one day we will dwell in that eternal place with God. I don't have all the answers, but I can have Jesus!

Chapter Ten

Questions and Answers

I believe that we should be lifelong students. We should always be learning, and we should always remain teachable. When I'm talking with someone who is more experienced in something than I am, it's a tremendous opportunity to "go to school" for a few moments. It expands our realm of thinking and wisdom can be gained in the process. I especially enjoy talking with people who have had incredible spiritual experiences. Their stories challenge me, they make my think, and they make me hungry for more of God.

This last chapter was my chance to ask a few question of Dan—to pick his brain on a few things. These moments were priceless to me, and I trust that as you read this chapter, you also will learn and grow. And in some ways, I hope that you are provoked—in a good way. Neither of us has all the answers, and if you were to ask the same questions a year from now, I doubt that the answers would be exactly the same.

At the conclusion of this chapter, Dan prayed a prayer of impartation that I believe was much anointed with the Holy

Spirit. We both have witnessed the power of impartations and we both have been the recipients of impartations. We believe that as you read this prayer you will sense the Spirit ministering to you — touching you, healing you, and restoring your passion and faith.

I know the value of prayers such as the one in this chapter. During a particular difficult season that my wife and I walked through, we prayed several prayers of declaration and impartation. We didn't just pray them once, but we declared them over our lives time and time again. The Bible exhorts us to pray in the Spirit (see Ephesians 6:18), and this prayer was prayed in the Spirit. Therefore, I believe that you can declare it over your life many times, and many times God will use the words of this prayer to minister to your life.

Rob: As we wrap up our time together, I want to ask you a few questions. What is the most common question that people ask you? As you travel from coast to coast, you meet hundreds — even thousands of people, so what is the most common question people ask you?

Dan: How did you learn the Word? I tell them that there are no shortcuts to learning the Word. You just have to immerse yourself in the Word. That would probably be the most common question I'm asked.

Rob: Tease that out a little bit. Do you read it, or do you listen to it?

Dan: When I drive, I listen to the Word in my Suburban on CD. I just want the Word to become flesh in me. I want the Word to read me and peel layers off me so that when I stand before people at a restaurant or stand before people in a church, I actually live God's message. I want to become one with the Word so that God can throw me out wherever He chooses. Now think about that for a moment. The Word is like seed. If I'm full of God's Word, then I'm full of His seed. The more seed that is in me the greater the potential I have in being used by God. So I read the Word and I listen to the Word. We have to live in the Word, Rob. We have to immerse ourselves in the Scripture. It's the only way to have it richly dwell in us.

Rob: What's your reading plan?

Dan: Whatever the Holy Spirit tells me. Sometimes I read the Bible through each month, and other times I focus on a theme. This year I'm reading the gospels and book of Acts through each week. Monday I read Matthew, Tuesday I read Mark, Wednesday I read Luke, and so on. So every week this year I've read Mathew, Mark, Luke, John, and Acts. I've lived in the gospels and

Acts to the point that I believe it's possible to live just like Jesus. His life and ministry have become familiar to me. But it changes, Rob. People don't need to do what I do, but they need to spend time soaking and studying the Scripture.

Rob: Second question, outside of the Word what are a few books that have touched you the most? What are some books that you would highly recommend?

Dan: E. M. Bounds books on prayer — all eight books have been put into one volume. I read that two or three times. Randy Clark's book that we talked about entitled *There is More* and Rick Renner's book *Dressed to Kill* on spiritual warfare were excellent. Renner's book has helped me greatly. Jon Ruthven's book *What's Wrong with Protestant Theology?* is a must read for anyone. I have read 1,500 books, Rob. It's hard to narrow it down to only a few.

Rob: Yes, I get that. We'll have a list of books in the Recommended Reading section of this book, too.

Dan: When I first got sanctified in 1995, I had such a hunger for God. When the Lord revealed to me that He purified my heart, I wanted to read books about that experience. So I developed a library of four hundred and some holiness classics, and I read them all. My favorite books at that time were written between 1860 and 1905 because those people were preaching with an authority and unction. They preached with an experience that they possessed themselves. It wasn't just a theology or some emotional euphoria, and it wasn't some mystical experience out in the future. It was something that was possible by faith now, and I really gleaned a lot from those who paved the way for us today. So I don't have favorite books, but some books have impacted me more than others. I'm looking for the next book to touch me, but I mostly enjoy the Bible.

Rob: Next question is what is your greatest personal challenge?

Dan: To stay eternally minded and not to let my mind become shaped by this world. I want to live and think from a kingdom perspective. That's the only way to live with the joy that is set before me, keeping my mind trained to think every moment with an eternal perspective. That's my personal challenge each day.

Rob: What is your greatest concern for the Church of Jesus Christ?

Dan: My greatest concern for the Church is that we would settle for a form of religion without a real intimate relationship with Jesus that results in love and power. I don't want to see the Church add Jesus to our busy lives rather than letting Him *become* our life. We are to be one with Him. I don't want to simply add Him on. He is to be the essence of who we are.

Rob: Amen. I agree. Here's a personal question. What do you do to relax? What do you do when you're not preaching to refresh yourself?

Dan: I have a pattern each day of resting in Jesus and renewing my spirit. I spend time with Jesus and allow Him to refresh my soul. But when I'm not traveling, there are two things I really like to do. First, I am really blessed to spend time with my grandchildren. Time spent with them always brings a refreshing to my spirit. Second, I really enjoy going to the mountains with my wife. I like to relax at the foot of the beautiful mountains and read books and my Bible.

Rob: Okay, one last question. What is the greatest lesson that you are learning? Maybe I could ask it this way: what has been the greatest lesson recently that the Holy Spirit has dropped into your life?

Dan: That is a multilevel question for me. I know that when I received this call to itinerant ministry, I preached messages about heart purity and entire sanctification. That message was largely embraced, but when I started preaching the results of being sanctified in terms of power and supernatural gifts, I received push back. I guess after that M-11 service where so many people criticized the move of God, it made me start doubting what our movement (the Church of the Nazarene) was about. What *is* our denomination about? Where are we heading if we don't want the manifest presence of God to come in power and glory? I thought about that long and hard for a while because it really bothered me.

Now I'm starting to realize that if I'm going to do this ministry that He's called me into, I have to walk in the center of God's heart. I have to become intimate with Him. The Lord is teaching me that my greatest responsibility is to keep a single perspective on Jesus. I cannot look at the culture, I cannot look at the Church or denomination, I cannot pay attention to what people say, but I have to keep my eyes fixed on Jesus because if my eyes are good, then my whole body is full of light. I like that verse in Matthew 6:22 that says, "The eye is a lamp of the body; so then if your eye is clear, your whole body will be full of light." As long as I look to Jesus, my entire body is full of His light, but if I get distracted and look to the right or left, then my spiritual life is hit and miss. I am filled with other things when my eyes are off Jesus.

So what I believe the Holy Spirit is teaching me these days is He has put the gifts in me through the Spirit, and He has given me a call to ministry. These gifts and calling are irrevocable (see Romans 11:29). He has placed His mantle on me to wake up the Church, and He told me that if I'll pursue that and that alone, He would back me up. I'm learning to keep my vision on Jesus and Jesus alone, and the more that I do that the more people are touched by Him. That is the main lesson I'm learning these days: keep my eyes on Jesus.

Rob: That's beautiful. Hebrews 12:2 says, "Fixing our eyes on Jesus, the author and perfecter of faith."

Dan: Amen.

Rob: I was reading that verse one time, and I realized something I hadn't seen before, and that is if I keep my eyes on Him, He will "perfect" or "finish" my faith. Who doesn't want perfect faith? Perhaps it's possible if we'll just keep our eyes on Jesus.

Dan: You know, Rob, I've had all these experiences and all these encounters with people. I have so many testimonies of what God has done, but everywhere I go people ask me how can we *learn* to live this? It seems like when people go to traditional Bible schools and colleges, they aren't taught to live in step with the Spirit and to live this kingdom life as expressed in the book of Acts. There are professors who use the word "kingdom" now and then, but they use it more in terms of physical needs or social justice. I'm talking about the kingdom coming to earth and making a transformational and even supernatural difference. I believe that when the kingdom comes, it touches our Spirit, body, and soul.

So what are we going to do about that, Rob? What is the Lord laying on your heart? How can we help people and train them how to live this kingdom lifestyle in our context of being Nazarene, Wesleyan, and Holiness people. In fact, how do we equip the entire Church of Jesus Christ to function in purity and power?

Rob: Several years ago, God called me to redig the wells in the Holiness movement. And that calling extends beyond the Church of the Nazarene to all churches in the Holiness movement. About three years ago, I organized Fire School Ministries. Through this ministry organization there are resources that will help pastors, leaders, and laypeople sustain a lifestyle of purity and power (those resources are available through our website: fireschoolministries.com).

God has also placed on my heart a call to start a ministry school, a Word and Spirit ministry school. This would be a school that teaches purity and power, a school that teaches holiness and healing. In 2016, we are launching weekend Fire School Intensives that will address some of the topics we have discussed in this book. We hope to livestream these intensives and most certainly the ministry school when it's started. Fire School will contain resources like this book that we are discussing today. But I have a burden to train people in the same biblical mandate that Jesus trained His followers in without compromising the message of holiness.

We plan to launch this ministry school here in Columbus, Ohio. This will be the home base, but I think eventually Fire School Ministries will have satellite schools all across the United States and internationally. We desire to have classes available for people to watch through video streams. Hopefully, some of those will soon be available on our website. This ministry is a Word and Spirit ministry, Dan. This is a ministry that will teach heart purity and a lifestyle of power. When I completed my dissertation, Dr. Daniel Ketchum said that he was unaware of any school in the United States with this focus. Are you aware of anything like Fire School Ministries?

Dan: No, I'm not aware of anything like that, Rob. Listen, I know that we are coming to the end of our joint effort of writing this book together. I want to end with this parting comment: I believe that God wants to heal, He wants to deliver, and He wants every person on this planet to be set free. I believe that He came to earth because He loves people and because He desires intimate fellowship with us. I believe in all the supernatural healings. All the physical and emotional healings are awesome and I love all the testimonies, but I really believe with the deepest conviction that the greatest healing one could ever receive is when they totally give their life over to Jesus Christ. That is the greatest transformation.

The most important experience a person can have is when they are not only forgiven of their sins, but they are sanctified, cleansed, purified, and filled with all the measure of God's glory and presence. All other healings are temporary, but the spiritual healing is eternal. It doesn't negate one from the other. Jesus went after both the temporary and eternal healings, but I believe that the mandate of the commission accounts require us to bring a message of eternal healing along with physical healing. One day when we all see Jesus, the only healing that is going to last is the internal spiritual healing of our hearts. The only thing that will matter is if we have yielded our lives completely over to God and become persons of faith.

Rob: Yes, that is so true, and I couldn't agree more.

Dan: So if what we are doing here today can help men, women, boys, and girls become people of faith, I want to do it more. Thank you for this opportunity, Rob, to talk with you. I have loved you these last five years. We talk every day so it is about time that we put something in writing.

Rob: Bless you, my friend. It is only appropriate that we close with a prayer of impartation. You know that people are going to be reading this book with desperate needs. In my mind, I picture someone reading this prayer of impartation, and the presence and the power of God touches them. You never know, this could be a life-transforming moment for someone. So with that in mind, I want you to pray, and I want you to pray believing that the Holy Spirit is going to take this and touch people all around the world with this prayer. Will you close with a prayer of impartation?

(As you read this prayer, open your heart up to the presence of the Holy Spirit. Believe that He desires to touch your life, and please send your testimony to us of what God did in this prayer of impartation so that we can rejoice with you.)

Dan: *Father God, I thank you for this time, I thank you for the experience of life that you have given to us, and I thank you that it is abundant, and that there is no end to your kingdom blessings. It is expanding forever. It is inside of us. I thank you, God, for those reading and listening to this prayer and for the hunger you put in their heart for more. They want to know you more, they want to live for you more, and they want to give you away more. Lord, I want to pray a prayer of impartation now for people to receive a greater measure of the Holy Spirit. And if they have not yet been sanctified, then I pray right now, God, that they would yield their life completely to you and receive the sanctification of their spirit, their soul, and their body. I believe that the power of your blood is enough to go all the way down to the depths of the sinner, and you can* *remove all sin, all depravity, and cleanse and sanctify them through and through. Lord, I pray for that man or that woman right now, that teenager, that boy, or that girl who is struggling with fear, or some kind of addiction, bondage, or depression. I pray right now in this prayer of impartation that they would be set free by the power of the Holy Spirit. Right now, God, I pray in this prayer that people would receive your calling to take the kingdom gospel around the world. I pray God that people would be healed right now. I declare that cancer, diabetes, dementia, heart conditions, every kind of illness, infirmity, sickness, and disease would be healed right now in this prayer. I pray that families would be reunited. That lost children and grandchildren would be found. I pray that marriages would be restored and broken relationships healed. Lord, I pray an impartation that no demonic force can have any sway over your children, here and now, in covenant with your name and your blood. God, we believe that there is no end to your government, there is no end to your kingdom, and we are carriers, we are ambassadors, and we represent your kingdom. And I pray that your kingdom would come and your will be done right now in the lives of everyone reading and hearing this prayer — just as it is in heaven. Unleash your power, unleash your love, unleash your glory, and may we never be the same. I pray this impartation in Jesus' name, amen.*

Rob: Amen!

Dan: We are done, Rob!

Conclusion

Becoming Love

I will never forget standing in a parking lot of a restaurant in Las Vegas about a mile from the strip, watching Dan prophesy and declare healing over the abused past of a waitress who had stepped out to smoke a cigarette. The contrast of that scene brought me to tears and moves me to this day. No more than a mile away people were being used and abused. The only real value placed on a person was the amount that they were willing to wager. Yet, amid that sex-driven, idolatress culture, the love of Jesus pierced through the veil of darkness and touched a young woman. Her name was Autumn, and when Dan finished praying, she said, "Thank you for truly loving me." Her response said it all. She had never encountered the love of Jesus like that. She had been used merely as an object of someone's gratification, but within a few moments she encountered the authentic divine love of God that still has power to transform lives.

There is a verse of Scripture that says, "For the love of Christ controls us" (2 Corinthians 5:14a). One commentator said that the word "control" means to be preoccupied with something.

What are you preoccupied with? Many of us have jobs, families, and bills, not to mention the array of responsibilities that come across our path. But is it possible to function in life and remain preoccupied by God's love? I believe we only need to look to Jesus for the answer. After washing the disciples' feet, Jesus said, "For I gave you an example that you also should do as I did to you" (John 13:15). Jesus came to serve, not to be served (see Mark 10:45). We're to have the same attitude as Him (see Philippians 2:5).

What I'm saying is that love should totally preoccupy our lives. Jesus concluded, "A new commandment I give to you, that you love one another, even as I have loved you, that you also love one another. By this all men will know that you are my disciples, if you have love for one another" (John 13:34–35). Think about that for a moment: the distinguishing characteristic of being Jesus' follower is how we love others. There is no greater impartation that we can give others than the love of Jesus. Autumn may not know much about Christianity, but this much for sure, she had an encounter with God's divine love that I believe will set her on a course to spiritual redemption.

You will never look into the eyes of someone who doesn't matter to Jesus, and you must see them as Jesus did: "distressed and dispirited like sheep without a shepherd" (Matthew 9:36b). I believe in the supernatural power of the Holy Spirit, and I believe that if we're filled with the Holy Spirit, we possess all nine manifestations found in 1 Corinthians 12:8–10. I believe God wants to use us to heal the sick, cast out demons, cleanse the lepers, and even raise the dead (see Matthew 10:8). But all of that activity is predicated on authentic love.

In fact, without love any supernatural activity will profit us nothing (see 1 Corinthians 13:3). We are to pursue love first and then desire the supernatural activity of the Holy Spirit (see 1 Corinthians 14:1). Of all the lessons that Dan and I are learning, nothing has been more profound and lasting than becoming love. Our prayer is that everyone reading this book will fall in love with Jesus once again, and being possessed with His love, you will allow that to be released upon everyone you lock eyes with.

Recommended Reading

Billman, Frank H. *The Supernatural Thread in Methodism: Signs and Wonders Among Methodists Then and Now.* Lake Mary, FL: Creation House Press, 2013.

Bounds, E. M. *E. M. Bounds on Prayer.* Grand Rapids, MI: Baker Books, 2004.

Brown, Michael L. *Authentic Fire.* Lake Mary, FL: Creation House, 2015

_____. *The Revival Answer Book.* Ventura, CA: Renew Books, 2001.

Bustin, G. T. *Dead: Yet… Live.* Westfield, Indiana: Fellowship Promoter Press, 1967.

Clark, Randy, ed. *Power, Holiness and Evangelism: Rediscovering God's Purity, Power, and Passion for the Lost.* Shippensburg, PA: Destiny Image Publishers, 1999.

_____. *Power to Heal.* Shippensburg, PA: Destiny Image, 2015.

_____, ed. *Supernatural Missions: The Impact of the Supernatural on World Missions.* Mechanicsburg, PA: Global Awakening, 2012.

_____. *There is More: The Secret to Experiencing God's Power to Change Your Life.* Minneapolis, MN: Chosen, 2013.

Cymbala, Jim. *Fresh Power: Experiencing the Vast Resources of the Spirit of God.* Grand Rapids, MI: Zondervan Publishing, 2001.

DeArteaga, William L. *Quenching the Spirit: Discover the Real Spirit Behind the Charismatic Controversy.* Lake Mary, FL: Creation House, 1996.

Dunn, James D. G. *Jesus and the Spirit.* Grand Rapids: Wm. B. Eerdmans Publishing Company, 1975.

Greig, Gary S., and Kevin N. Springer, eds. *The Kingdom and the Power.* Ventura, CA: Regal Books, 1993.

Hughey, Rhonda. *Desperate for His Presence: God's Design to Transform Your Life and Your City.* Bloomington, MN: Bethany House Publishers, 2004.

Jernigan, C. B. *Pioneer Days of the Holiness Movement in the Southwest.* Kansas City, MO: Nazarene Publishing House, 1919.

Johnson, Bill, and Randy Clark. *The Essential Guide to Healing: Equipping All Christians to Pray for the Sick.* Bloomington, Minnesota: Chosen Books, 2011.

Nathan, Rich, and Ken Wilson. *Empowered Evangelicals: Bringing Together the Best of the Evangelical and Charismatic Worlds.* Boise, ID: Ampelon Publishing, 2009.

Ravenhill, Leonard. *Why Revival Tarries.* Minneapolis, MN: Bethany House Publishers, 1982.

Rench, Craig W. *The Master's Plan: A Strategy for Making Disciples.* Kansas City, MO: Beacon Hill Press, 2011.

Renner, Rick. *Dressed to Kill: A Biblical Approach to Spiritual Warfare and Armor.* Tulsa, OK: Teach All Nations, 2007.

Ruthven, Jon Mark. *What's Wrong with Protestant Theology: Traditional Theology Versus Biblical Emphasis.* Tulsa, OK: Word and Spirit Press, 2013.

Teykl, Terry. *The Presence Based Church.* Muncie, IN: Prayer Point Press, 2003.

Wagner, C. Peter. *This Changes Everything: How God Can Transform Your Mind and Change Your Life.* Ventura, CA: Regal Books, 2013.

Becoming Love Ministries Association

Since 2008, Dan Bohi has been answering the Lord's call to awaken the church of Jesus Christ to the power, purity, and freedom of the Spirit-filled life, found, realized, experienced and exhibited in the lives of believers in the book of Acts. He has traversed the country from coast to coast crossing denominational lines teaching the timeless truths from God's Word. Pastors and church leaders have confirmed that thousands have experienced encounters with the presence of God in his meetings and congregations have been transformed.

To help fulfill the call to awaken churches, Dan founded an international ministry called, Becoming Love Ministries Association (BLMA). This ministry is now comprised of a team of fulltime ministers and evangelists who help impart kingdom truths through writing, leading, training, equipping, and traveling across the nations holding crusades and conferences in denominations and churches of all sizes. Becoming Love is more than the name of this ministry; it is the spring from which life and ministry flows forth.

Rob McCorkle, who travels fulltime with BLMA, wrote a power-packed book that explains how the Word and the Spirit became separated and why people discount for supernatural. Without compromising the truths of God's Word, Rob calls all believers to lives of holiness while exploring how the supernatural power of the Holy Spirit should accompany one who is consecrated to Christ. Learn why biblical Christianity is the fusion of purity and power — the marriage of the Word with

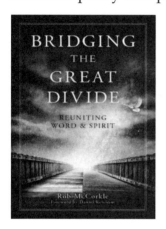

the Spirit. Discover anew Jesus' call to a lifestyle of intimacy with Him and how from that posture you can become a student of the Word and a practitioner of the Spirit. This book will both provoke and encourage you. As you journey through the Bible, history, theology, and practical stories, you will end up next to Jesus.

For team booking, information, or resources please contact:

Jim Williams (Executive Director)
7905 North West 48th Street
Bethany, OK 73008
jimwilliams@becomingloveministries.com
BecomingLoveMinistries.com
BecomingLoveLibrary.com

ENDNOTES

1   Jim Cymbala, *Storm: Hearing Jesus for the Times We Live In* (Grand Rapids, MI: Zondervan, 2014), 74.

2   Ibid.

3   S. B. Shaw, ed., *Echoes of the General Holiness Assembly* (Chicago, IL: Shaw Publisher, 1901), 73.

4   Jim Cymbala, *Fresh Power* (Grand Rapids, MI: Zondervan, 2001), 81.

5   John Wesley, *The Works of John Wesley* (Kansas City, MO: Beacon Hill Press, 1986), 499–500.

6   Steve Beard, *Thunderstruck: John Wesley and the Toronto Blessing* (Wilmore, KY: Thunderstruck Communications, 1996), 3.

7   John Telford, ed., *The Letters of John Wesley* (London: The Epworth Press, 1931), 303.

8   Vinson Synan, *The Century of the Holy Spirit: 100 years of Pentecostal and Charismatic Renewal* (Nashville, TN: Thomas Nelson, 2001), 204.

9   Ibid.

10 Stephen A. Seamands, "The Great Divorce: How Power and Purity Got Separated." In Randy Clark, ed., *Power, Holiness and Evangelism* (Shippensburg, PA: Destiny Image Publishers, 1999), 121.

11 Frank H. Billman, *The Supernatural Thread in Methodism: Signs and Wonders Among Methodists Then and Now* (Lake Mary, FL: Creation House Press, 2013), 70. For more detail, see Vinson Synan, *The Holiness-Pentecostal Tradition* (Grand Rapids, MI: Eerdmans Publishing Company, 1971, 1997).

12 Seamands, "The Great Divorce," 131–132.